The
A to Z of Elizabethan London

Compiled by

Adrian Prockter and Robert Taylor

Introductory notes by

John Fisher

HARRY MARGARY, LYMPNE CASTLE, KENT
in association with Guildhall Library, London
1979

ISBN 0 903541 28 9

Printed in Great Britain by Headley Brothers Ltd The Invicta Press Ashford Kent and London

CONTENTS

INTRODUCTION

What was London like four hundred years ago? The answer is provided by a wide range of contemporary sources such as John Stow's *Survey of London* published in 1598, Henry Machyn's diary (1550–63), and Van den Wyngaerde's drawings, as well as by paintings, property plans and archaeological remains. But perhaps nothing gives a better overall impression than the three map-views reproduced on the following pages. These are the earliest printed maps of our capital city. Compiled at the beginning of Queen Elizabeth I's reign with primitive surveying equipment,[1] they are nevertheless remarkably accurate and informative documents and merit close study, preferably with a magnifying glass. Not only do they show a vast amount of purely topographical detail, they also depict Elizabethan Londoners at work and at play. The detail is so fine—especially on the incomplete Copperplate Map—that such seemingly insignificant features as garden wells, rowing boats, weathervanes, wine barrels, dogs, and laundry baskets are discernible. The maps even show us what kinds of clothes people wore.

With the exception of certain areas on the 'Agas' woodcut map, all three map-views have reasonably consistent horizontal scales. However, unlike modern two-dimensional Ordnance Survey plans, every detail is shown in bird's-eye perspective. The principal drawback with this type of map is that some of the smaller streets are obscured by neighbouring houses. But there is one important advantage: it is possible to observe the appearance of a large number of buildings and other topographical features.[2]

Before examining what the maps show in greater detail it is necessary to discuss briefly how the three map-views were compiled and the relationship between them, since this has a bearing on the degree of confidence we can place in their accuracy. Only a summary of the evidence and the theories is given here, and more detailed discussion of dating and authorship will be found in Marks (1964)*, Darlington & Howgego (1964), and Holmes (1966).

The Copperplate Map

It is now generally accepted that the so-called 'Agas' woodcut map-view on a scale of about 28 inches : 1 mile (*c.*1:2260) and the smaller engraving by Frans Hogenberg on a scale of 6½ inches : 1 mile (*c.*1:9750) are both derived from a much larger, more detailed and more accurate original engraved on fifteen copper plates by an unknown artist[3] at a scale of about 34 inches : 1 mile (*c.*1:1860). The total size of this original map must have been somewhere in the region of 3'8" by 7'5" (112 cm. by 226 cm.). Disappointingly, only two of the fifteen plates are known to have survived (one in a private collection and one in the Museum of London) and no printed copies exist. The two plates are contiguous and cover a north-south section of London extending from Shoreditch to London Bridge. An important clue to the date of the Copperplate Map is provided by the topographical detail on the two surviving plates, which, to summarize a mass of evidence, points to the period 1553–1559. One researcher has recently produced evidence which suggests that the surveyor was at work after 1557.[4]

Braun and Hogenberg's Map

Frans Hogenberg's engraved map-view entitled 'Londinum Feracissimi Angliae Regni Metropolis' first appeared in Volume 1 of Braun and Hogenberg's atlas *Civitates Orbis Terrarum*. Although this was published in Germany in 1572 the map clearly shows London at an earlier date, as St. Paul's Cathedral is shown complete with its spire which was destroyed by lightning in 1561. Comparison of the spelling and the incidental detail on this map with the anonymous Copperplate Map leads one to the conclusion that Braun and Hogenberg's map-view is merely a reduced copy of the complete Copperplate Map, on one sheet. It is extremely well engraved, and, despite its much smaller scale, reveals more detail than one might expect.

---

* A list of the books and maps referred to in the text is given on page xii. 'Agas' map references are given by the grid square (e.g. 3N) followed where necessary by an oblique stroke and the code number of the object (e.g. X73).

The 'Agas' Map

Unlike its two companions, the so-called 'Agas' map-view is a woodcut, of which only three impressions have survived—one in Guildhall Library, one in the Public Record Office, and one in the Pepysian Library at Magdalene College, Cambridge. It is printed on eight sheets, the total size of the map being about 2′4″ by 6′0″ (71 cm. by 183 cm.). Unfortunately the sections do not fit together particularly well and it is obvious that the edges of the printed sheets and the wooden blocks themselves must have been damaged at some stage. The original width of the map must have been at least 6′2″ (188 cm.). Whereas Braun and Hogenberg and the Copperplate Map show nothing north of Shoreditch, the 'Agas' woodcut extends as far as the hills of Hampstead and Highgate. Beyond the built-up area the angle of view gradually decreases, and the scale is progressively compressed so that at the northern edge the map becomes a true panorama. The scale is similarly but less obviously distorted on the south side of the river, presumably for the purpose of fitting in Lambeth Palace. Although the arms of James I appear in the top left-hand corner of the three extant 'Agas' maps, this is clearly a later insertion, and in fact the State Barge shown near Baynard's Castle (6L/X182) bears the Tudor royal arms. The map must have originally been produced at some time between 1561 and 1570, first because St. Paul's spire is not shown (it will be remembered that this was destroyed in 1561) and secondly because one of the woodblocks has clearly been altered to show the new Royal Exchange, completed in 1570. It is possible that the 'Agas' map is the 'Carde of London' which was entered in the Stationers' Registers by Giles Godhed, a printer and purveyor of woodcuts, in 1562–3. Once again many of the incidental details on the map, such as the basket carriers in Moorfields (3Q/X53), demonstrate that the woodcut, too, was largely based on the anonymous Copperplate Map. A rather inferior copy of the woodcut, engraved on pewter and commonly referred to as Vertue's map, was produced at the end of the seventeenth century. Strangely the Tudor arms appear in the corner and the Royal Exchange is not shown, which indicates that it must have been copied from the original state of the 'Agas' map.

How the Elizabethan surveyor Ralph Agas (1545–1621) ever came to be associated with the woodcut is a mystery, since it bears absolutely no relation to his usual cartographic style, and Agas was too young to have compiled it in any case. The confusion seems to have arisen in the eighteenth century when George Vertue misinterpreted some lines of doggerel on Ralph Agas's map of Oxford concerning a proposed map of London—lines which in fact imply that Agas had *not* produced a map of London by 1588. Ralph Agas's name is now so firmly linked with the woodcut that to re-name it would probably make matters even more confusing.

The three map-views compared

The three map-views are therefore complementary. Generally speaking the Copperplate Map is the most detailed and reliable of the three but it covers only part of the City. The 'Agas' woodcut, which is on almost the same scale as the Copperplate Map, has the advantage of being complete but is more crudely executed: compare for example object X73 in square 3N with the same feature on sheet 1 of the Copperplate Map. Braun and Hogenberg's map probably follows the original survey more closely than 'Agas' but is engraved on a much smaller scale with consequent loss of detail.

Elizabethan London

Looking at the maps as a whole, one's first impression of early Elizabethan London is that it was a relatively small and compact city. Its population of about 100,000, served by over 100 churches, was packed into an area barely exceeding one square mile (c.2.6 km²). By today's standards there was little suburban sprawl, and the wall—still intact at this period—acted as a sharp dividing line between town and country on the northern and eastern sides of the City. Access to the commercial heart of London could only be gained via London Bridge (one of the wonders of the Tudor world) or through one of the principal City gates, some of which were decorated with the decaying heads and limbs of traitors, impaled on spikes (cf. Moorgate and Bishopsgate on plate 1 of the Copperplate Map). The official boundary of London was marked by barriers known as the 'bars', most of which are indicated on the maps (e.g. Aldgate Bars, 4V).

Westminster, the seat of government and the site of the royal palace of Whitehall, was still a separate community, linked to the City of London by the Thames and the Strand, along which stood some particularly large and splendid residences. Beyond the City in all directions lay hedged fields where cows, horses, and one or two very peculiar crossbreeds can be seen grazing peacefully. Rivers such as the Fleet (2H) and Tyburn (visible only in the bottom left-hand corner of Braun and Hogenberg) can be seen winding their way past villages like Islington (1J) and St. Giles (3C), and a network of sluggish streams and drainage ditches in Lambeth and Finsbury betrays the presence of extensive tracts of marshland, parts of which were used for dumping refuse.

Churches

Looking more closely at the buildings on the two large-scale map-views, the question that immediately springs to mind is: how accurately are they depicted? We can certainly sympathize with the engravers for not having bothered to show each individual house exactly as it appeared; many have been left out, and much detail has been glossed over, particularly on 'Agas'. But it would be a mistake to suppose that the mapmaker merely surveyed the streets and used his imagination to fill in the intervening spaces. Whilst many of the humbler domestic buildings may be drawn conventionally, this cannot be said to apply to the more important secular and ecclesiastical buildings.

With only a few exceptions, every church that existed in London in the mid-sixteenth century is shown in its correct position.[5] Churches known from other contemporary sources to have had tall spires, such as St. Dunstan in the East (6S) and St. Lawrence Poultney (6Q/N), are depicted with tall spires on the maps, and the representation of the tower of St. Mary-le-Bow (4M) corresponds very closely to an impression on a brass seal engraved for the parish churchwardens in 1580. Indeed, every church tower appears to be drawn slightly differently—horizontal hatching on St. Matthew Friday Street (4M) could, for instance, indicate that it was made of wood—and it is tempting to suppose that incidental details such as louvres, stair turrets, weathervanes and crosses are all authentic. But this would probably be going too far. St. Mary Aldermary (5N/3) *must* be drawn conventionally, if one accepts John Stow's statement (1598) that the tower was only 16 to 20 feet high at the time the maps were compiled. Neither is it easy to reconcile some of the churches on the maps with those shown in the Wyngaerde sketches,[6] though there is a remarkable similarity in a number of cases (cf. St. Martin Vintry; 6N/Y).

It is therefore only possible to draw the conclusion that whereas churches are generally depicted truthfully on the Copperplate Map, the degree of accuracy varies from place to place and the map must always be used critically. It should also be remembered that 'Agas' seldom follows the Copperplate Map very closely and must therefore be used with even more caution. For example, 'Agas' shows a number of church towers without naves, yet there is no evidence to suggest that these churches were in a ruined condition at the time. In at least one instance 'Agas' is inferior to Braun and Hogenberg: the circular plan of the Temple Church (5G) is apparent only on the smaller-scale map.

Monastic remains

When Elizabeth I came to the throne the face of London was changing almost as dramatically as it is today. In the quarter-century following the dissolution of the religious houses by King Henry VIII, the fabric of monastic London had been gradually disintegrating, yet the maps provide clear evidence that much remained. It is possible to pick out the cloisters of the Black (Dominican) Friars (5K/X86), White (Carmelite) Friars (6H) and Grey (Franciscan) Friars (4K/X126), the magnificent church of the Austin Friars (4Q) which had been granted to the Dutch in 1550, and the remains of Holy Trinity Priory, Aldgate (4S)— once the most splendid monastic foundation in the City. Much monastic property passed into the hands of wealthy and influential men who sometimes converted the principal buildings into luxurious town houses. Two such individuals were Sir Edward North, who came into possession of the Charterhouse (previously a Carthusian priory) in 1544 (2K), and the Marquis of Winchester, who built Winchester House on part of the Austin Friars' estate (3Q). Other ex-religious property was demolished to provide building materials, taken over for industrial purposes (glass kilns, storehouses, etc.) or simply converted into tenements. Despite some ambiguities,[7] the mid-sixteenth century map-views are of great value in that they often provide the only visual record of these intriguing monastic remains.

Secular buildings

Like the churches, many of the important secular buildings with distinctive architectural features stand out clearly from the masses of more conventionally drawn timber-framed houses. Again the detail is often remarkable, but one cannot always rely on its authenticity; the eastern part of the Tower of London (6V) is, for instance, drawn very inaccurately on both 'Agas' and Braun and Hogenberg, and the Tower as a whole is not shown in its correct position relative to the City wall.

Besides William the Conqueror's massive fortress guarding the approaches to the City, the largest complex of buildings in the Elizabethan capital was the royal palace of Whitehall (6B), which occupied about 23 acres (c.9.3 hectares) between St. James's Park and the river. It consisted of numerous courtyards and ornamental gardens, all shown more or less in their correct positions. As for the appearance of the palace buildings, it is interesting here to compare 'Agas' and Braun and Hogenberg with a sketch by Wyngaerde made around 1550, reproduced in Barker and Jackson (1974). There appears to be some degree of correspondence, but not very much, and it is evident that on 'Agas' the Holbein Gate (6B/X79) has been depicted with greater care than the Cockpit (6A/X102). Due south we come to Westminster Abbey and the

remains of the royal palace of Westminster (7A), severely damaged by fire in 1512, where Parliament and the Law Courts sat. At first sight these buildings may appear to be crudely engraved, but closer inspection reveals that the artist has actually gone to the trouble of depicting the flying buttresses on Westminster Hall. On the north shore of the Thames between Westminster and the City lay a number of private palaces. Many of these had once belonged to bishops and were similar in function and appearance to Lambeth Palace (8C), now the sole survivor. Lambeth Palace is more faithfully delineated on Braun and Hogenberg than on 'Agas', who does not appear to show the gatehouse or the great hall. To the east of the belt of land occupied by the law schools of the Inner and Middle Temple lay the royal palace of Bridewell (6J), built by Henry VIII—who only spent an occasional night there in the 1520s—and later presented to the City by Edward VI as a workhouse.

Within the City walls the most important secular buildings were the Guildhall (4N)—London's own seat of government—and the halls of the livery companies, successors of the medieval guilds. Forty-nine companies had halls at this time. Not all were purpose-built, but the wealthiest and most influential companies owned very imposing premises with extensive gardens. Three such companies were the Drapers, whose turreted hall can be clearly seen in Throgmorton Street (4Q); the Mercers, whose hall stood in Cheapside (4N); and the Fishmongers who occupied a building near London Bridge (6R). Only a few livery halls are readily identifiable on the maps, but in compiling the present Index it was thought useful to indicate the sites of those halls whose locations are known with certainty. From 1570 onwards the hub of commercial activity in the City was the Royal Exchange, which was modelled on the Bourse at Antwerp. It is only shown on 'Agas' (4Q). On top of this building is perhaps the strangest object on the whole map (X50). It looks rather like an oil-can, but is in fact intended to be a grasshopper—the crest of Sir Thomas Gresham, founder of the Exchange.

Houses

Whoever was responsible for producing the Copperplate Map made no attempt to show every house in London. This can be verified by comparing the two copperplates with contemporary property plans drawn on a larger scale. As a rule, the cruder 'Agas' map omits even more buildings than the Copperplate Map; for example on the north side of Leadenhall Street (4S) between St. Mary Axe and St. Katherine Cree, 'Agas' shows eight distinct houses compared with ten on the Copperplate Map. (Twenty-three are shown on Leake's survey of 1666 and thirty-three on Ogilby and Morgan's plan of 1676.) Likewise, most buildings on the map-views appear to consist of only two storeys when in fact there were probably three or four. However, as Martin Holmes (1969) has pointed out, the cartographer does occasionally show interesting details such as the posts and crossbars used for supporting display counters outside shops (visible in Cheapside on the Copperplate Map), and the pentice above the ground floor windows which sheltered goods on show. Even some climbing plants can be seen growing on a trellis in the back garden of a house in Bucklersbury (5P/X150). In spite of the fact that the map-views show only a proportion of the total number of buildings that existed in Elizabethan London, it is unlikely that this ratio varies much from place to place, so that we are able to compare the density of housing in different parts of the city. Very little open space is to be seen amongst the warehouses and tenements between Lombard Street and the river front, but gardens become increasingly evident as one moves northwards and eastwards where land was marshy and of less value.

Water supply

London's rapidly growing population naturally depended on an efficient supply of food and water. Piped water to individual homes was at this time virtually unknown, but pipes did run from springs in the north-western suburbs along the Strand to conduits in Cheapside (4N/W17). Most people had their water delivered to them by professional water-carriers who obtained supplies either directly from the Thames or from street pumps and wells in enormous wooden 'cans' which looked not unlike milk churns. Two such waterbearers can be seen wading about in the Thames replenishing containers strapped to the backs of ponies (7P/P26; 6T/P6), and groups of water-cans can actually be seen standing beside the conduits in Cheapside (4N/X11; 4L/W1). At least twenty-five wells, pumps, conduits, etc. are visible on the 'Agas' map. Many others are shown on the Copperplate Map but they are often tucked away in gardens and are not easily spotted. Surprisingly, one or two of the more important sources of water are omitted on all three maps, for example Bishopsgate Conduit.

Food markets

The maps provide rather less evidence of markets. 'Agas', for instance, does not depict the trestle tables set up in the middle of Long Southwark (8R) as Visscher does in his 1616 panorama. However, in square 5P we notice the Stocks Market (now the site of the Mansion House) where fish and meat could be purchased, and in square 3K can be seen the great livestock mart of Smithfield. Railings and sheds indicate the site of

Newgate Market (4K/X64). In the quadrangle of Leadenhall, formerly a large mansion but later converted into a market for poultry and other commodities, it is possible to pick out the scales that were used for weighing meal (5R/X191). Perhaps most interesting of all is a row of stalls stacked together in the centre of Cheapside (4N/W17), much as they would be in any market town today.

Industry

In the sixteenth century, as now, London was an industrial centre of great importance. On the north side of Houndsditch, for example, there was a gun foundry, delightfully referred to as 'Ye Goounefowuders' on Braun and Hogenberg's map, and represented by a small cannon (4T/X2). A similar factory can be seen at the corner of Water Lane and Thames Street (6T/X1). Rather more obnoxious were the brick and lime kilns, belching smoke in every direction. One is shown near Goswell Road (1L/X14), and another was situated in Scotland Yard, alarmingly close to the Palace of Whitehall (5C/X25). The maps also remind us of the kinds of power supply used in sixteenth-century London, such as wind and water. Three watermills can be seen on the Southwark shore, built over streams discharging into the Thames (7J/X116; 8U/X111; 7V/X108). Looking northwards from Moorgate, an Elizabethan Londoner would have noticed on the horizon a group of windmills situated on top of rubbish tips in Finsbury Fields (2P). These post-mills are particularly clearly depicted on the Copperplate Map; a hooded sack-hoist can even be seen, which would suggest that they were used for grinding corn rather than for pumping water out of the surrounding marsh as has sometimes been assumed. It should be mentioned in passing that 'Agas' is more accurate than the Copperplate Map in showing three instead of two windmills on the north side of Hog Lane. Another activity to be observed is the drying and stretching of cloth on racks known as tenter frames. The 'Agas' map indicates that the tenter grounds were concentrated near the City wall, especially around Houndsditch and Fore Street (3S; 3N). The large open spaces on the north side of London, from Moorfields in the east to St. Martin's Field in the west, were used regularly by laundresses who laid their washing out on the ground to bleach and dry, occasionally pegging down large items to prevent them from blowing away (3Q/X16).

Commerce and trade

As the hub of commerce and trade in England, London's position was unrivalled. Braun and Hogenberg choose to portray a typical London merchant, wearing a long fur-trimmed gown and flat woollen cap, in the lower margin of their map, and people in similar costume can be seen walking about in Finsbury Fields on the Copperplate Map. Naturally the river front was the focal point of London life, and a variety of ships—barges, herring-busses, deep sea 'barks' and galleons—can be seen moored in the 'Pool' below the Bridge. Many of the 'legal quays' that had been appointed by Act of Parliament in 1559 are named on 'Agas', and a number of cranes are visible on the waterfront (6N). They appear to be mounted on axles rather like the post-mills in Finsbury Fields. Although the maps do not show much activity on the quays themselves, the names of the wharves often reflect the types of commodity that were unloaded and stored, viz. Fish Wharf, Salt Wharf, Vintry Wharf, Timberhithe and Hay Wharf. Goods being transported down the Thames such as timber and hay were generally unloaded above the Bridge, whereas ships from the Continent docked between the Bridge and St. Katherines.[8] The German Hanse merchants had their headquarters at the Steelyard (6P), in the middle of which can be seen a curious tower (X193) of a kind found in other ports such as King's Lynn. Perhaps this was used for keeping an eye on the movements of shipping. Well away from the river, just north of the church of St. Bartholomew the Great, is a vacant plot of land (3K/X179). This was the site of the annual Bartholomew Fair, at this time the most important cloth fair in the kingdom.

It must be remembered that although the maps give us a good idea of the range of commercial and industrial activities taking place in mid-sixteenth century London, there is much that they do *not* show. Stow, for instance, informs us that Lothbury (4P) was full of foundries, which apparently made a 'loathsome noise to the by-passers'. By plotting the additional topographical information contained in Stow's *Survey* directly on to the 'Agas' map, a much fuller and more realistic picture of the Elizabethan City can be built up.

Recreation and entertainment

What did Londoners do in their spare time? Once again the maps provide plenty of clues. Archery must have been particularly popular, for scattered about Finsbury Fields we can see groups of men in short cassocks armed with bows and arrows. These archers strolled around the fields—which have been compared to a modern suburban golf course—shooting at a series of 'marks' or stakes, doing their best to avoid

passing pedestrians, grazing cattle and the occasional milkmaid (2U/P2). The targets were usually decorated wooden posts set in the hedgerows and two such 'marks' actually survived *in situ* until the end of the nineteenth century. Not surprisingly accidents were common. Dame Alice Owen founded a school at Islington in gratitude for a narrow escape when a stray arrow passed through her hat. Somewhat less fortunate was a woman mentioned in Machyn's *Diary* who was 'slayne gohyng in Finsbere feld with her husband with an arow shott in the neke'. Thankfully musketry was practised behind a brick wall (2S/P24).

Other forms of recreation are visible on the south side of the river. Near Barge House Stairs a couple can be seen taking their dog for a walk along the dyke which separated Lambeth Marsh from the Thames (7G/P1). Further east, in the area known as Paris Garden, we notice what appears to be a wayside cross (7J/X55). Martin Holmes (1969) has suggested that this could be a quintain—a horizontal paddle-shaped crossbar pivoted on an upright post which was used as a target by riders armed with a lance or staff. It is true that the object on Braun and Hogenberg's map looks more like a quintain than a cross, and Braun and Hogenberg are often more reliable than 'Agas', but this might just be an example of carelessness on the part of the engraver. Approaching Southwark we come to Bankside—a suburb notorious for its brothels or 'stews' (8P/X216) and shortly to become famous as the site of Shakespeare's Globe playhouse. Here stood the Bull Ring and Bear Garden (8M; 8N)—two circular arenas where Londoners could enjoy the blood-thirsty spectacle of bulls and bears being attacked by savage mastiffs. The dogs were kept in kennels adjoining each arena, and they can be seen straining at their leashes (8M/X118). East of London Bridge refreshment could be obtained at a 'Beere Howse' (8V), and a similar establishment can be seen on the opposite side of the river (visible only on Braun and Hogenberg). Ale houses and inns were of course far more numerous than the maps suggest. Perhaps it was at these two particular taverns that the mapmaker revived himself after spending a tiring day surveying the city.

More colourful forms of entertainment took place at Whitehall, where Queen Elizabeth and her Court resided for much of the year. Within the grounds of the palace there was a tilt-yard 'for noblemen and others to exercise themselves in jousting' (6B/X37), several tennis courts (6A/X130; X151; X127), a bowling alley (6A/X201) and a cock pit (6A/X102). The entertainment which probably drew the greatest crowds of all was the occasional public execution on Tower Hill. It was here, for instance, that the Lord Protector Somerset met his end in 1552. The scaffold and gallows are clearly discernible on both Braun and Hogenberg and 'Agas' (5T/X65), and gallows are also depicted on Braun and Hogenberg's map just south of Charing Cross. In Smithfield, however, there is nothing to remind us of the four years of terror during Mary's reign (1554–58) when 43 Protestants were burnt at the stake.

Transport

Visitors to Elizabethan London must have experienced difficulty finding their way around the city, as there were no horse-drawn vehicles for hire, and it was not possible to purchase pocket-maps to guide one through the maze of narrow, twisting lanes. In fact the most convenient means of getting from one side of London to the other was by boat, the River Thames serving as a kind of 'urban motorway'. Instead of making for the nearest 'bus stop or underground station, the traveller would have walked briskly to the nearest jetty or 'stairs', where a waterman would have been waiting to ferry him to his destination. There were about 2,000 rowing boats or 'river taxis' plying up and down the Thames, and no less than 57 are shown on the 'Agas' map. A serious drawback with this mode of travel was the presence of London Bridge, whose nineteen piers and 'starlings' severely obstructed the flow of the river, causing a great deal of turbulence. Unless one was prepared to risk one's life (not everybody got away with just a soaking), it was advisable to disembark and by-pass the Bridge on foot. Amongst the many oared vessels shown on the 'Agas' and Braun and Hogenberg maps there is one of particular interest. It is in fact the Royal Barge being towed upstream to Whitehall Palace by a galley (6L/X182), and steered with a long sweep. The Queen is surrounded by a guard of halberdiers.

Streets

It is when studying the street pattern on the three maps that the principal disadvantage of the 'map-view' becomes apparent. By drawing the buildings in elevation a large proportion of the smaller alleys and courtyards are obscured, and one only needs to look at the large scale plan of the City produced in 1676 by John Ogilby to discover just how many of these small streets existed. To describe Elizabethan London as a rabbit warren would probably be an understatement. The main streets, however, are generally drawn with remarkable accuracy. Lime Street (5R) and Basinghall Street (4N) follow the same twisting courses shown on the current Ordnance Survey map. The only areas where there appears to be a serious distortion and confusion are in the neighbourhood of Blackfriars (5K), St. Lawrence Poultney (6Q) and St. Giles in the Fields (3C)—where the street pattern bears little resemblance to a larger map of the area drawn up by Ralph Treswell in 1585.

Conclusion

Like so many historical documents these early printed maps of London need to be used with a certain amount of caution. Bearing in mind that they probably represent the first attempt at mapping the whole of London, some omissions and inaccuracies are inevitably present. Yet despite their deficiencies they present a most informative and generally reliable record of Elizabethan London. No better surveys were produced until over a century later when, following the Great Fire of 1666, John Ogilby and his step-grandson William Morgan completed the first true large-scale plans of the capital.

REFERENCES

1. Rapid developments were taking place in surveying methods during the middle and latter part of the sixteenth century. A useful introduction to Elizabethan surveying equipment and techniques will be found in A. W. Richeson's *English Land Measuring to 1800: Instruments and Practices* (Cambridge, Mass.: M.I.T. Press, 1966).

2. By far the finest map-view ever published was Wenceslaus Hollar's etching of West-Central London, *c*.1658, reproduced by the London Topographical Society in 1908 (publication number 12). This undoubtedly formed part of Hollar's projected 'Great Map' of London and Westminster which he was in the process of compiling between *c*.1658 and 1666 when the Great Fire rendered large parts of it obsolete. The Great Map was never completed and only the 'West-Central' sheet was published. Map-views went out of fashion around 1700, though later maps sometimes show important buildings in elevation.

3. According to R. A. Skelton (personal communication) the orthography of the names on this map suggests that the engraver was Flemish or Dutch.

4. At the corner of Billiter Lane and Fenchurch Street the Copperplate Map shows a distinctive block of three tenements, three and a half storeys high, and clearly taller than its neighbours. The Court Books and Accounts of the Clothworkers' Company show that this block was rebuilt four and a half storeys high in 1557, and it can be reconstructed from a plan and survey of 1612. Since the houses on the Copperplate Map are generally drawn at least one storey lower than they must have been in reality, it seems reasonable to suppose that the tenements shown are the ones erected in 1557. Buildings on the site before 1557 are not known but they would almost certainly not have reached such a height. I am indebted to Mr. John Schofield for bringing this to my attention.

5. There were 106 churches in the City in the mid-sixteenth century. Sixty-three *should* appear on the two copperplates, but five are omitted: St. Leonard Eastcheap, St. Mary-at-Hill, St. Nicholas Acon, St. Stephen Coleman and St. Mary Colechurch. The same churches are omitted on 'Agas', as well as others. The Copperplate Map and 'Agas' both show St. Martin Orgar in the wrong place and include an extra tower in Watling Street.

6. Three sketches by A. van den Wyngaerde in the Ashmolean Museum, Oxford. Reproduced in Barker and Jackson (1974). See also Wyngaerde's 'View of London *c*.1550', reproduced in the same book.

7. In the case of the Charterhouse it is not clear whether 'Agas' shows the church, part of the cloister, or North's Great Hall.

8. The drawbridge in the centre of London Bridge was raised for the last time in 1500.

ACKNOWLEDGEMENTS

The Index has been compiled by Adrian Prockter. The task of plotting the overlaid information on to the maps has been undertaken by Robert Taylor. The following people helped to identify features on the map and offered advice: Dr. Caroline Barron, Victor Belcher, Mary Boast, Howard Colvin, Anthony Dyson, Rhoda Edwards, Philippa Glanville, H. J. M. Green, Vanessa Harding, Daphne Hart, J. L. Howgego, Ralph Hyde, Lord Miles of Blackfriars, Dr. Ann Saunders, John Schofield, and Rosemary Weinstein. Their very valuable assistance, and that of the local history librarians in the Borough Libraries in the area covered by the 'Agas' map, is acknowledged with much gratitude.

The *A to Z of Elizabethan London* has been published under two imprints, that of the London Topographical Society and that of Harry Margary in association with Guildhall Library. Mr. Margary has designed the book and seen it through the press; the Society is most grateful to him for all his expert knowledge and zealous labours.

The base-map used for the 'Agas' sheets in the present publication has been reproduced from LTS Publication No. 17.

1. *General histories of Tudor London*

Baker (Timothy): *Medieval London* (London: Cassell, 1970).

Barker (Felix) and Jackson (Peter): *London; 2000 years of a city and its people* (London: Cassell, 1974). Chapter 3 deals with Tudor London.

Borer (Mary Cathcart): *The City of London: A history* (London: Constable, 1977). Chapters 7 and 8 deal with Tudor London.

Holmes (Martin R.): *Elizabethan London* (London: Cassell, 1969).

2. *Contemporary descriptions of Tudor London*

Kingsford (C. L.), editor: *John Stow. A survey of London. 1603.* 2 vols. (Oxford: Clarendon Press, 1908).

Nichols (J. G.): *The diary of Henry Machyn, 1550–1563* (Camden Society, 1848).

3. *Dictionaries of London streets and buildings*

Ekwall (Eilert): *Street names of the City of London* (Oxford: Clarendon Press, 1954).

Harben (Henry A.): *A dictionary of London* (London: Jenkins, 1918). Deals only with the City.

Wheatley (A. B.) and Cunningham (P.): *London past and present.* 3 vols. (London: Murray, 1891).

4. *Works about the three map-views*

Darlington (I.) and Howgego (J.): *Printed maps of London c.1553–1850* (London: Philip, 1964). New edition published by Dawson in 1979.

Holmes (Martin R.): *Moorfields in 1559* (London: H.M.S.O., 1963).

Holmes (Martin R.): 'A source book for Stow?' in *Studies in London History*, ed. by A. E. J. Hollaender and William Kellaway (London: Hodder & Stoughton, 1969), pp. 257-85. In this paper the author sets out to demonstrate that John Stow compiled his *Survey* using the Copperplate Map as an aid.

Holmes (Martin R.): 'An unrecorded map of London'. *Archaeologia*, vol. 100 (1966), pp. 105-128.

Marks (Stephen): *The map of mid-sixteenth century London* (London: London Topographical Society, 1964).

5. *London's Roman remains*

Merrifield (Ralph): *The Roman City of London* (London: Benn, 1965).

6. *Maps and panoramas*

Horsleydown, *c.*1544. A copy of this manuscript plan is held by the Southwark Local Studies Library.

Leake (John) and others: *An exact surveigh of the streets . . . contained within the ruines of the City of London . . . 1666* (L.T.S. publications nos. 22 and 26).

Morgan (William): *London etc. actually surveyed*, 1682 (Facsimile published 1977 by Harry Margary in association with Guildhall Library).

Norden (John): *London* and *Westminster* 1593 (L.T.S. publication no. 7). Map-views from *Speculum Britanniae*.

Norden (John): *The View of London Bridge from east to west*, 1597 (L.T.S. publication no. 45).

Ogilby (John) and Morgan (William). *A large and accurate map of the City of London*, 1676 (Facsimile published 1976 by Harry Margary in association with Guildhall Library).

Rocque (John): *A plan of the cities of London and Westminster and Borough of Southwark*, 1746 (Facsimile published 1971 by Harry Margary).

Seventeenth-century plans of properties belonging to St. Bartholomew's Hospital (L.T.S. publications nos. 83, 84, 87, 88).

Treswell (Ralph): Geldings Close, 1585 (L.T.S. publication no. 54). Shows area between Bond Street and Long Acre.

Treswell (Ralph): Survey of property belonging to the Clothworkers' Company, 1612 (L.T.S. publications 72-75).

Vertue (George): *Civitas Londinum Ano Dni Circiter MDLX*, 1737. The unsigned version of Vertue's map appears to be a crude copy of the original state of the 'Agas' woodcut, no examples of which have survived.

Visscher (C. J.): View of London 1616 (L.T.S. publication No. 4). Also reproduced in Barker and Jackson (1974).

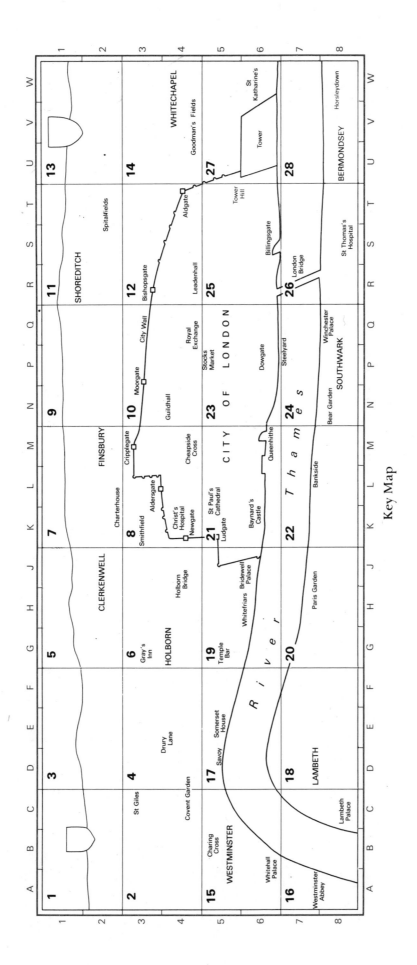

Key Map

1

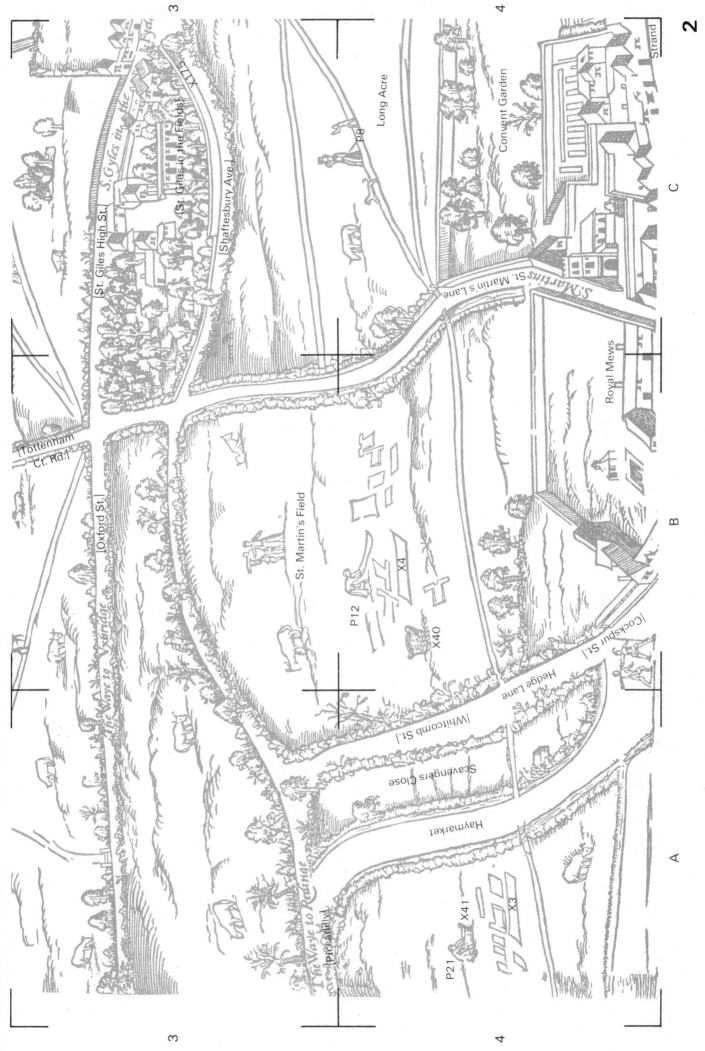

Strand

C

Convent Garden

Long Acre

P8

St. Giles in the Fee

3

St. Martins St. Martin's Lane

[St. Giles High St.]

[St. Giles in the Fields]

[Shaftesbury Ave.]

X15

Royal Mews

[Tottenham Ct. Rd.]

[Oxford St.]

The Way to Uxbridge

B

St. Martin's Field

P12

X4

X40

[Cockspur St.]

Hedge Lane

[Whitcomb St.]

Scavengers Close

Haymarket

The Way to Reading

[Piccadilly]

A

P21

X41

X3

3

4

3

4

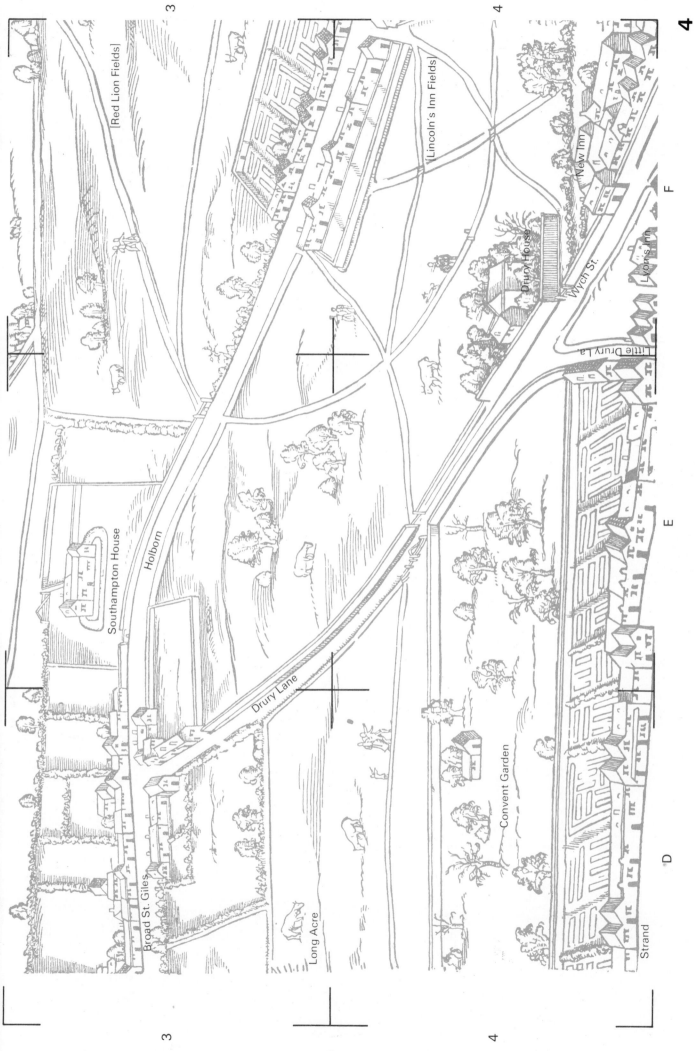

[Red Lion Fields]

3

[Lincoln's Inn Fields]

Southampton House

Holborn

Drury House

Wych St.

New Inn

4

Broad St. Giles

Drury Lane

Little Drury La.

Lyon's Inn

Long Acre

Convent Garden

Strand

D

E

F

3

4

Islington

J

H

G

1

2

(Clerkenwell

Clerken Well

St. Mary

Nunnery pt.

St. James

X167

W3

Clerkenwell Green

(Turnmill

St.

St. John St.

Clerkenwell Rd.

St. John, Priory of

X124

Farringdon Rd.

Fleet River

Townsend La.

Hockley in the Hole

Clerkenwell Rd.

P16

Grays Inn Rd.

1

2

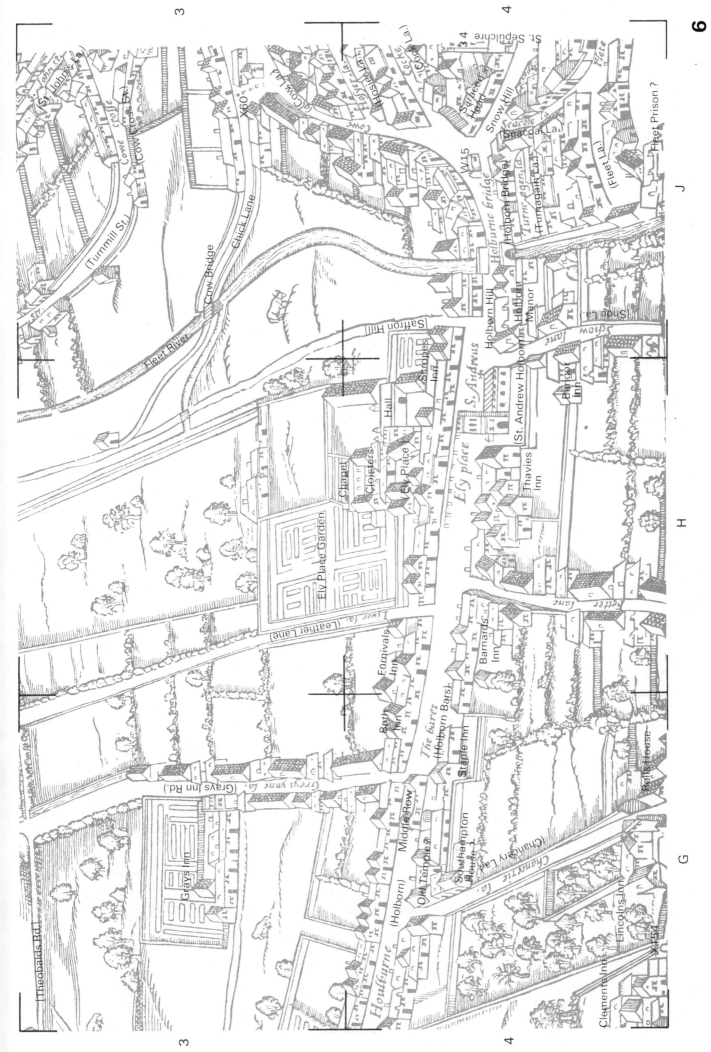

3

4

St. Sepulchre

3 4

Snow Hill

Sarscen's
Head

W15

(Holborn Bridge)

(Cock La.)
(Cock La.)
(Hosier La.)
(Hosier La.)

X60

Cow La.
Cow La.

(St. John's La.)

Cowe
Crosse

(Cow Cross St.)

(Turnmill St.)

Cow Bridge

Chick Lane

Fleet River

Saffron Hill

Scrobes
Inn

Hall

(Ely Place N.)

Cloisters

Chapel

Ely Place Garden

(Leather Lane)

Liver La.

Furnivals
Inn

Bath
Inn

(Grays Inn Rd.)

Grays Inn

Grays Inne La.

Middle Row

Old Temple ?

Southampton
House ?

(Holborn)

Houlburne

The Bares
(Holborn Bars)

Staple Inn

Barnards
Inn

(Chancery La.)

Chancerie

Clements Inn

Lincolns Inn

X154

Rolls House

Fetter Lane

Shoe La.
Shoe La.

Bangor
Inn

Thavies
Inn

(St. Andrew Holborn)

Ely place

S. Andrews

Holborn Hill

Holborn
Manor

Holborn Hill

Holburne bridge

Turne agente

(Turnagain La.)

(Seacoal La.)
Seacole

(Fleet La.)

Flete

Fleet Prison ?

J

H

G

[Theobalds Rd.]

3

4

7

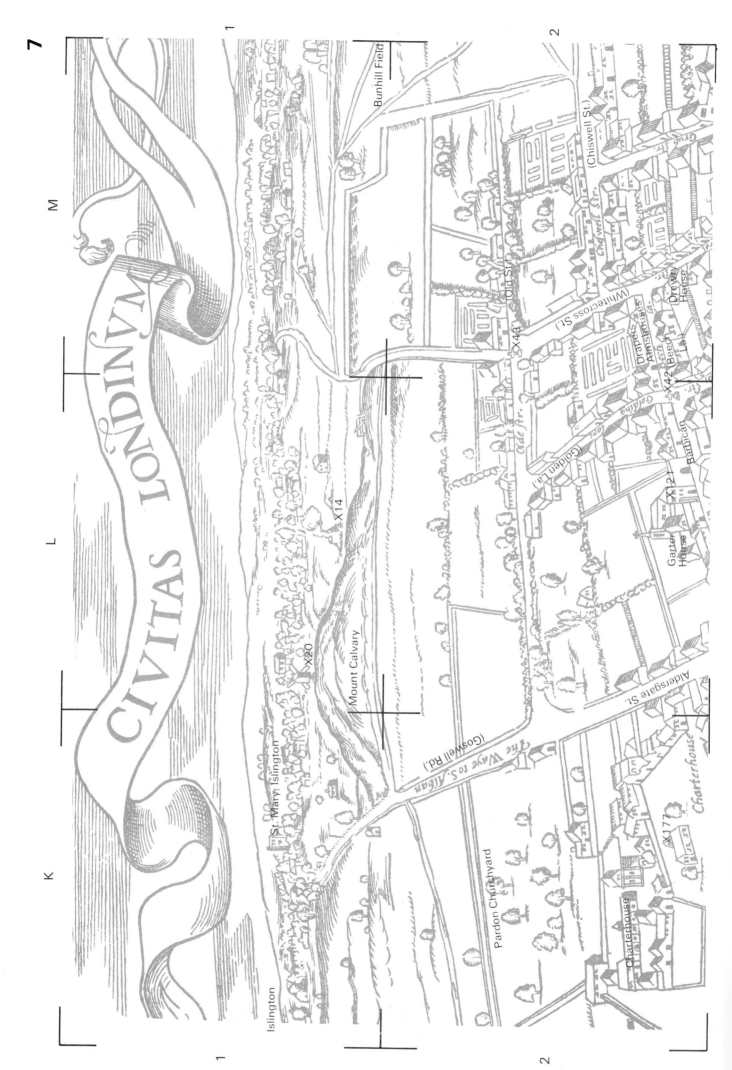

CIVITAS LONDINVM

Islington

St. Mary, Islington

X14

X20

Mount Calvary

Pardon Churchyard

Charterhouse

X17

Charterhouse

Aldersgate St.

(Goswell Rd.)

The Waye to S. Alban

(Golden La.)

Olde Str.

Garter House

X121

Barbican

(Golden La.)

Drapers Almshouses

X42 Beech La.)

Drewry House

X43

(Old Str.)

(Whitecross St.)

Chiswell Str.

(Chiswell St.)

Bunhill Field

K L M

7

8

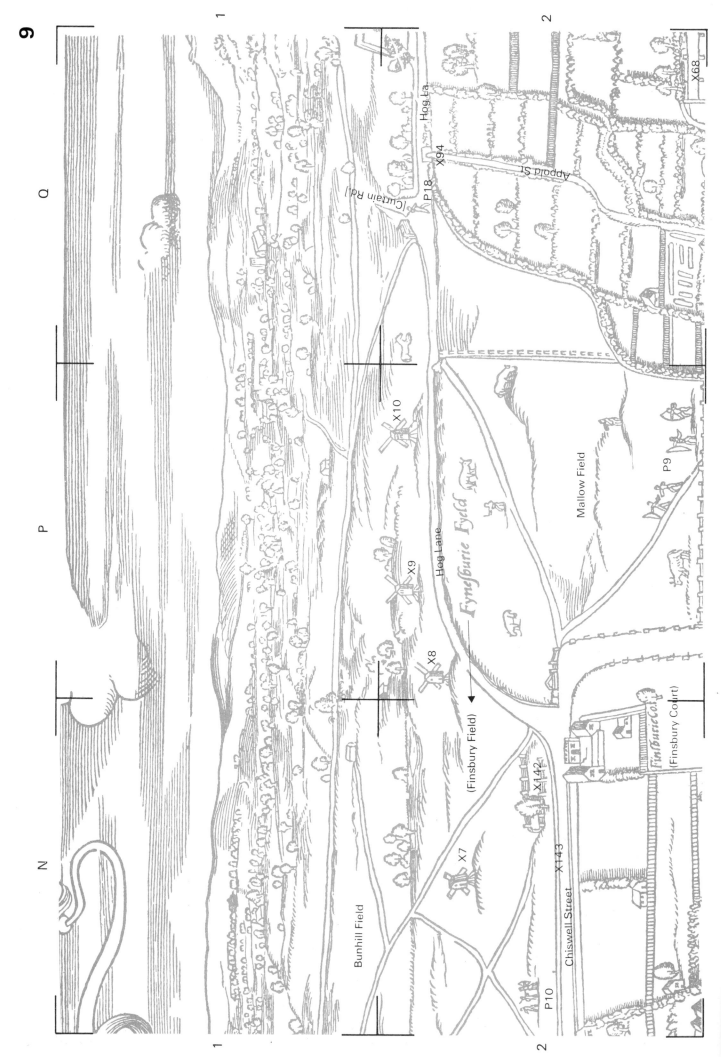

N   P   Q

1

Bunhill Field

X7

X142

X143

X8

X9

X10

Hog Lane

[Curtain Rd.]

P18

X94

Hog. La.

Fynesburie Fyeld

(Finsbury Field)

Mallow Field

P9

FinsBurie Co.

(Finsbury Court)

P10

Chiswell Street

Appold St.

X68

2

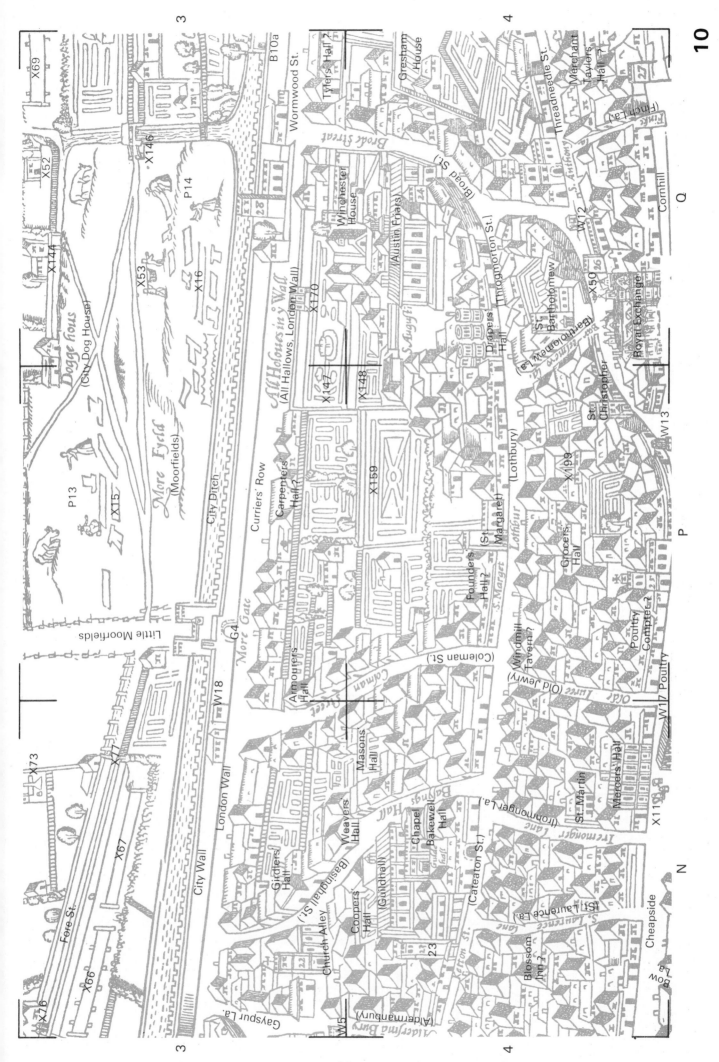

T

S

R

The Spui Fyell
(Spitalfields)

P17

P15

X74

X75

P24

Artillery Yard

X82

X171

St. Mary Spital

Tassell
Close

Hog La.

Shoreditch

St. Leonard

Norton
Folgate

Shordich
(Shoreditch)

(Bishopsgate)

Bishoppis gate streete

W10

Hog La.

Hog La.

X68

1

1

2

2

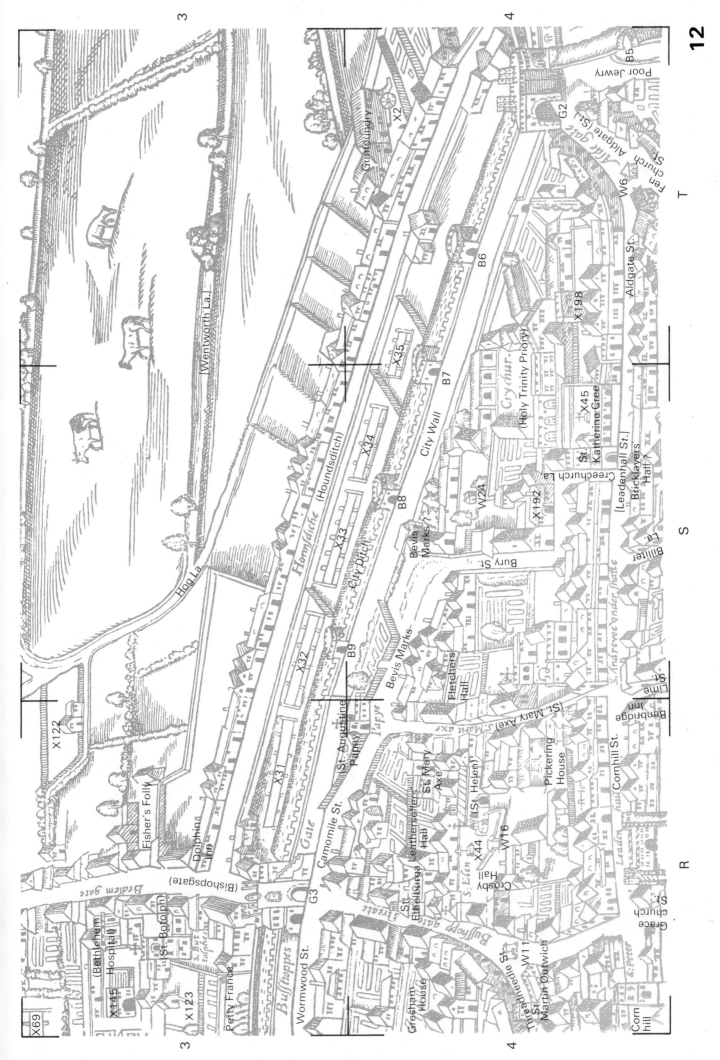

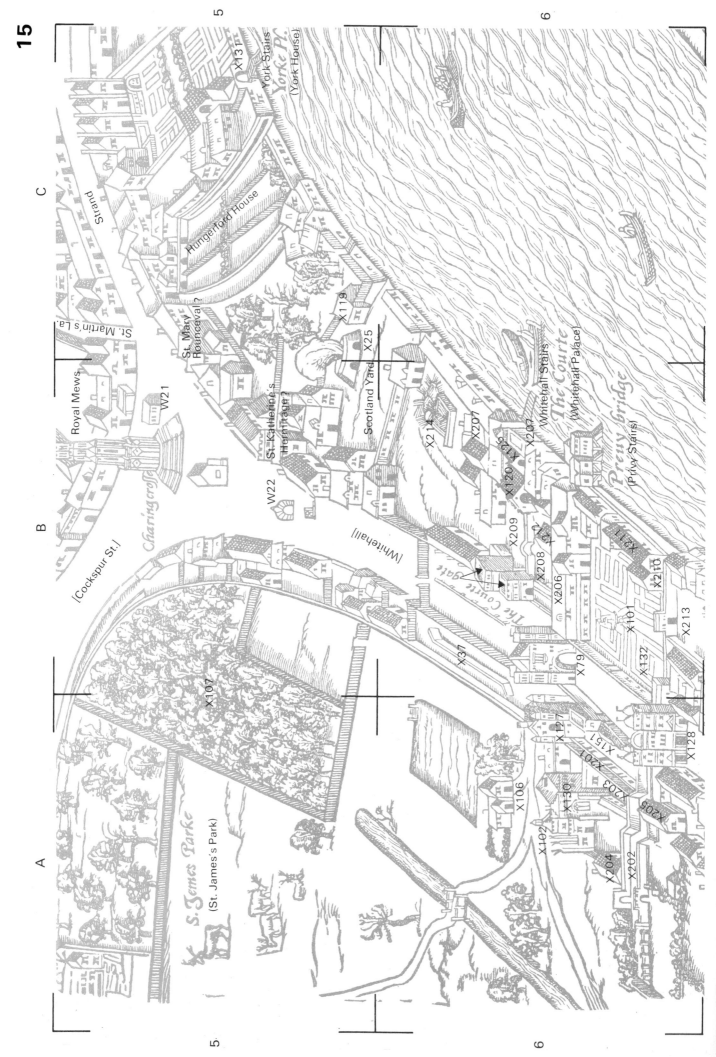

A

B

C

5

6

S. Iemes Parke
(St. James's Park)

[Cockspur St.]

Charingcrosse

Royal Mews

St. Martin's La.

Strand

W21

W22

St. Mary
Rounceval?

St. Katherine's
Hermitage?

Hungerford House

York Stairs
Yorke Pl.
(York House)

X131

X119

X25

Scotland Yard

[Whitehall]

X107

X31

X106

X127

X151

X201

X203

X205

X204

X202

X102

X130

X128

X213

X132

X101

X79

X210

X211

X206

X208

X207

X209

X212

X120

X125

X207

X214

Whitehall Stairs

The Courte
(Whitehall Palace)

Preuy Bridge
(Privy Stairs)

The Courte Gate

5

6

Narrow Wall

P19

Lambeth Marsh

X39

X38

St. Mary

Lambeth Palace

[Lambeth Road]

The Lambeth

Stangate Stairs

Westminster Stairs

X180

Horse Ferry

Chanou Row
(Cannon Row)

Starre Chamber

(Star Chamber)

Westminster Palace

The Queens bridge
(Queen's Bridge)

W20

(Westminster Hall)

X104

X92

Westmynster hall

X97

X105

X98

X103

X99

The olde Palaice

X100

Kinges Streate (King St.)

X96

X166

St. Margaret

Westmynster

Westminster Abbey

Westminster School

A

B

C

Butcher Row

X165

X153

Mylforth la.
(Milford La.)

Arundel Place
(Arundel House)

Holywell St.

F

X85

Lyon ƒtm

W23

Little Drury

Strand la
(Strand La.)

E

Strand

Somerset Place
(Somerset House)

X167

B

Bedford House

Sauoye
(Savoy Palace)

D

Ivy benche
(Ivy Bridge La.)

Narrow Wall

Durƒme Pl
(Durham House)

THis antient and famous City of London, was firſt founded by *Brute* the Trojan, in the year of the World two thouſand, eight hundred thirty & two, and before the Nativity of our Saviour Chriſt, one thouſand, one hundred, and 30. So that ſince the firſt building, it is 2 thouſand 7 hundred 60 & 3 years. And afterward was repaired & enlarged by King *Lud.* but at this preſent ſo flouriſheth, that it containeth in length from the Eaſt to the Weſt about 3. Engliſh miles, from the North to the South about 2 Engliſh miles. It is alſo ſo plentifully peopled, that it is divided into a hundred and 22. Pariſhes within the Liberties, beſides 16 Pariſhes that are in the ſuburbs. It is planted on a very good ſoyle: for on the one ſide it is compaſſed with corne & paſture ground, and on the other ſide it is incloſed with the river of Thames, which not only aboundeth in all kind of freſh water-fiſh, but alſo is ſo navigable, that it as well bringeth abundance of commodities from all parts of the World, as alſo convcieth forth ſuch commodities as the plentifulneſſe of our Contry doth yeild us: which both augments the fame therof abroad, and alſo increaſeth the riches thereof at hom; ſo that as it is head and chief City of the whole Realm, ſo is it likewiſe head and chief Chamber of the whole Realm, as well for our outward as inward commodities. God proſper it at his pleaſure. Amen.

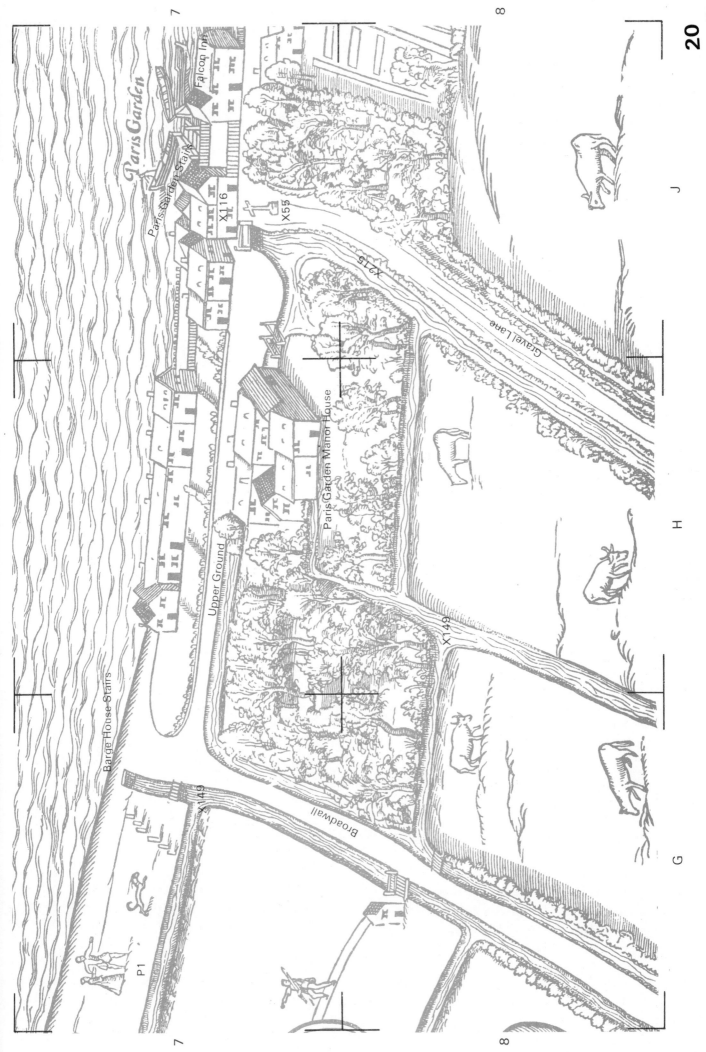

Paris Garden

Falcon Inn

Paris Garden Stairs

X116

X55

X275

Gravel Lane

Paris Garden Manor House

Upper Ground

X149

Barge House Stairs

X149

Broadwall

P1

J

H

G

7

8

7

8

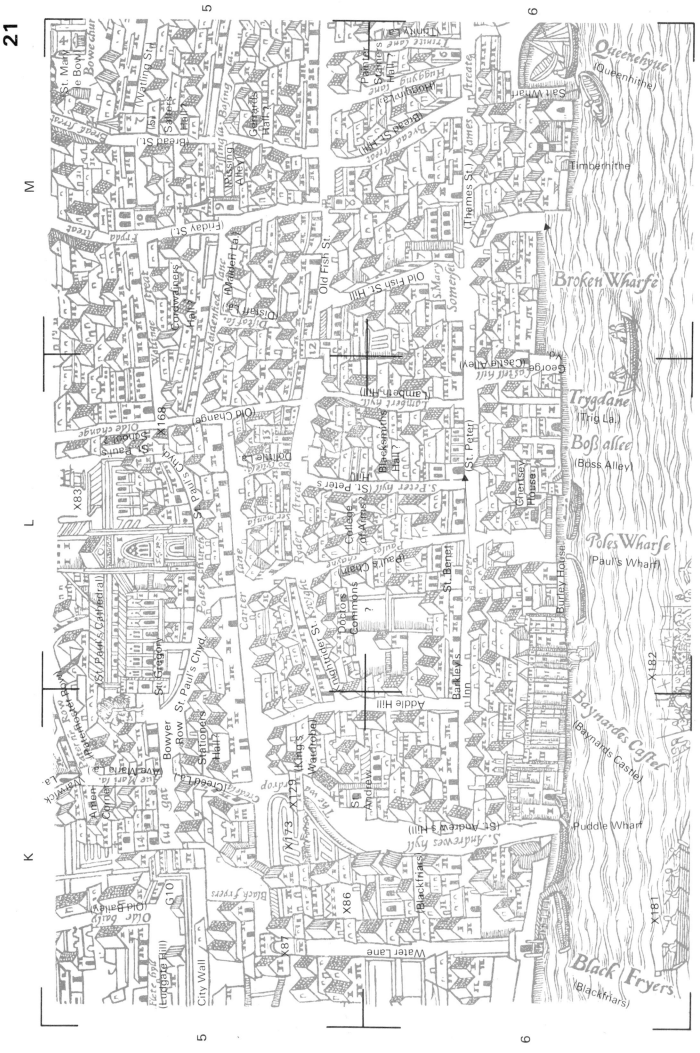

X117

X117

X117

X118

X172

The Banck (Bankside)

The bolle bayting
(Bull Baiting)

X117

X118

Pike Garden

Molestrand Dock

X182

X183

Falcon Stairs

M

L

K

7

8

8

7

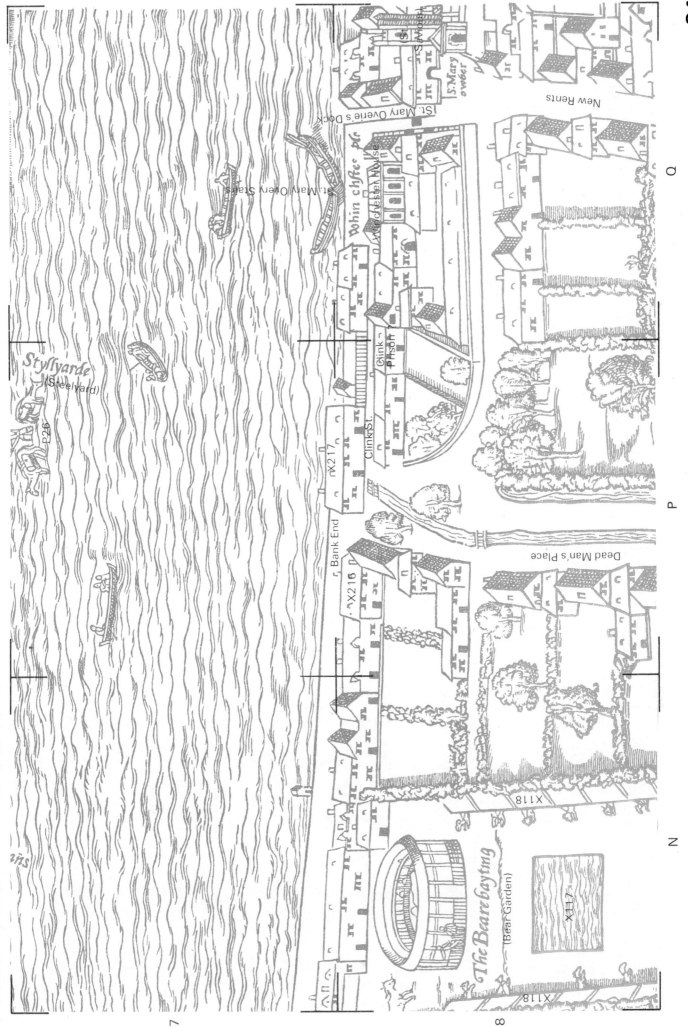

Styllyarde
(Steelyard)

P26

St. Mary Overy Stairs

St. Mary Overie's Dock

St. Mary Overie

S.t
Savioui

New Rents

Q

Winchester House

Whin chfee pte

Clink
Prison

Clink St.

X217

Bank End

X216

Dead Man's Place

P

The Bearebayting

(Bear Garden)

X118

X117

X118

N

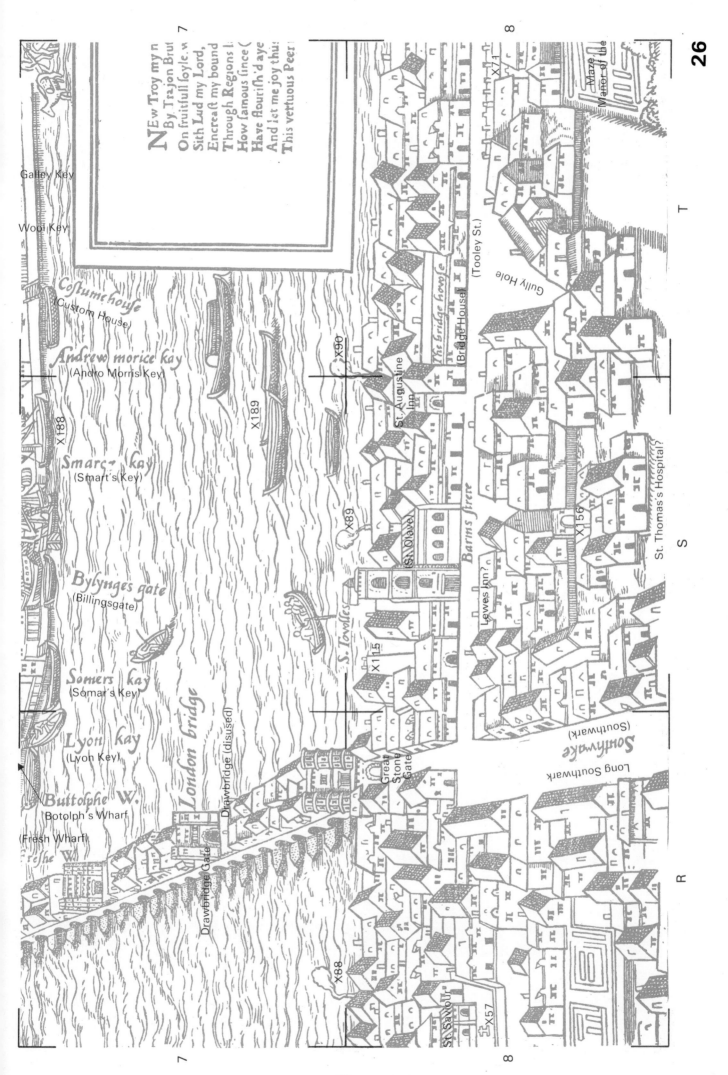

NEw Troy my n
By Trajon Brut
On fruitfull foyle. v 7
Sith Lud my Lord,
Encreaſt my bound
Through Regions l
How famous ſince (
Have flouriſh'd aye
And let me joy thus
This vertuous Peer

Galley Key

Wool Key

Coſtume houſe
(Custom House)

Andrew morice kay
(Andro Morris Key)

X188

Smarci kay
(Smart's Key)

Bylynges gate
(Billingsgate)

Somers kay
(Somar's Key)

Lyon kay
(Lyon Key)

Buttolphe W.
Botolph's Wharf

(Fresh Wharf)

reſhe W

London bridge

Drawbridge Gate

Drawbridge (disused)

X189

X90

X89

S. Towlles

X115

St. Olave

Barms ſtreet

St. Augustine Inn

The Bridge houſe
(Bridge House)

(Tooley St.)

Gully Hole

Lewes Inn?

X156

St. Thomas's Hospital?

Maze
Manor of the

Southwake
(Southwark)

Long Southwark

Great Stone Gate

X88

St. Saviour

X57

X71

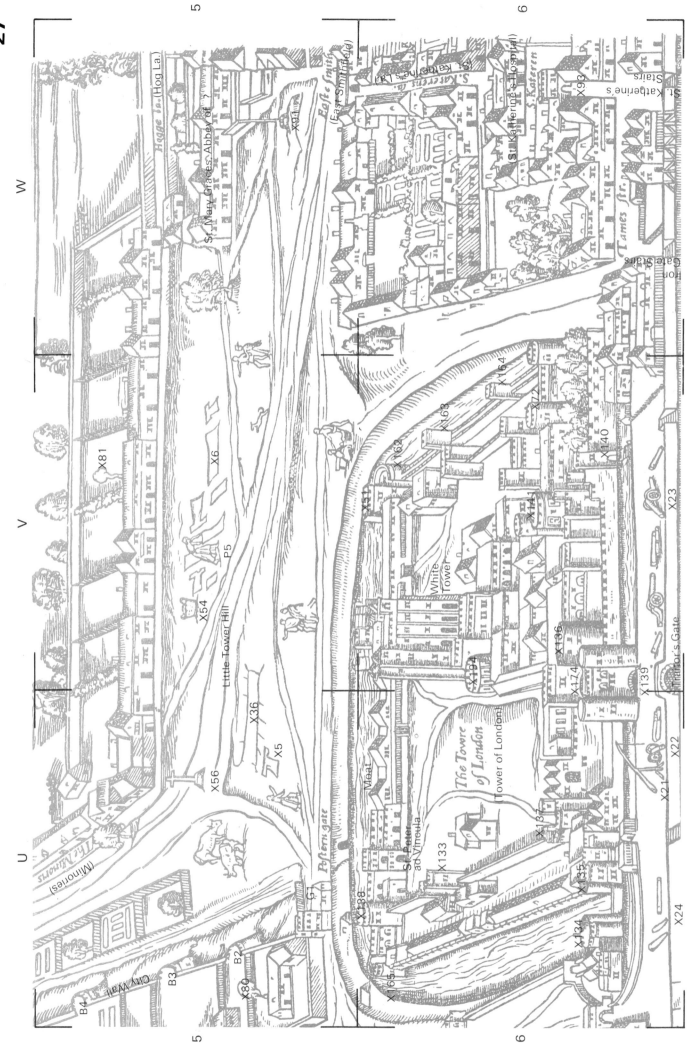

W

V

U

5

6

Hogge la. (Hog La.)

St. Mary Graces Abbey of ?

X81

X6

P5

X54

Little Tower Hill

X36

X5

X56

B2

B3

B4

City Wall

The Minories (Minories)

X80

G7

Postern gate

Balie smith (East Smithfield)

X61

S. Katerens la. (St. Katherine's La.)

S. Katerens

(St Katherine's Hospital)

X93

St. Katherine's Stairs

Iron Gate Stairs

Tames str.

X164

X163

X162

X72

X140

X51

X141

White Tower

X23

X136

X194

X174

X139

Traitor's Gate

X22

X21

X24

Moat

The Towre of London (Tower of London)

St. Peter ad Vincula

X133

X137

X135

X134

X165

X138

5

6

CP1

The Copperplate Map (North section)—CP1

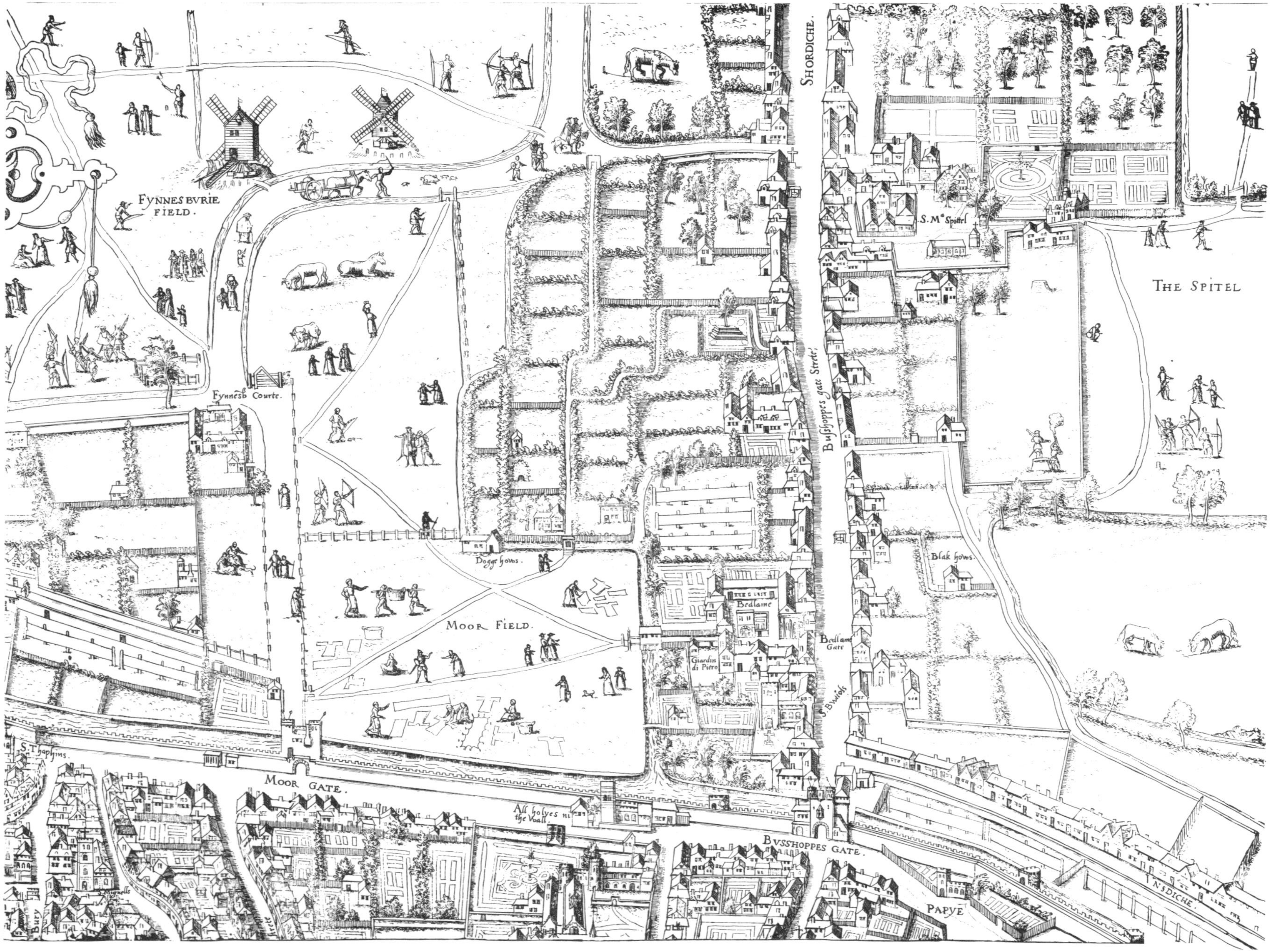
FYNNESBVRIE FIELD.
Fynnesb Courte.
SHORDICHE.
S.Mʳ Spittel
THE SPITEL
Busshoppes gate Strete
Blak hows
Dogge hows.
MOOR FIELD.
Bedlame
Bedlam Gate
Giardin di Pitro
S. Buttols
S.T haphins.
MOOR GATE.
All holyes in the Voall
BVSSHOPPES GATE.
PAPYE
NSDICHE.
Bury

The Copperplate Map (South section)—CP2

The Braun and Hogenberg Map—BH

EXPLANATION OF THE INDEX

A few reference numbers and letters actually appear on the 'Agas' map, and it seems reasonable to suppose that a key originally existed. No such key has survived. To remedy the deficiency and to aid interpretation, the present much larger Index has been compiled.

In general only buildings and objects that can be definitely identified on the map are listed in the Index. However, certain livery halls, inns, and prisons, even when not clearly distinguished on the map, have been included where their locations are known with certainty.

The Index entries provide the following information:

(1) The place name, or the name of the object featured. For City place names the spelling adopted is generally that of Harben in his *Dictionary of London*. When a place name is enclosed in square brackets this indicates that it is a present-day name and was not in use in the sixteenth century.

(2) The map reference. Code numbers appear in round brackets immediately after the place name. References to the 'Agas' map indicate grid squares (e.g. 3P); references to the Copperplate Map appear as CE1 (for the upper plate) and CE2 (for the lower plate); references to Braun and Hogenberg's map are indicated by the letters BH, the reader being advised to locate the place required by reference first to the 'Agas' map. 'Agas' map references in round brackets indicate the grid square in which the feature should appear.

(3) The spelling of the name as it is expressed on the 'Agas' map, on the Copperplate Map, and on the Braun and Hogenberg map.

(4) Brief notes. Because of the complexity of the subject, no attempt has been made to indicate every variant spelling or to give the derivation of place names. For this information one is referred to Harben and Ekwall (see 'Further Reading'). Present-day names are provided when they differ.

On the 'Agas' map place names are overprinted in red, except in those instances where the names on the original map are entirely unambiguous. Overprinted names in round brackets represent spellings as used in the Index. Overprinted names in square brackets represent present-day names that were not in use in the sixteenth century.

PLACE NAME INDEX

ABCHURCH LANE — 5Q CE2 BH
Abchurche lane; Abchurche 1; —

ADDLE HILL, THAMES STREET — 6K BH
Called 'Adlestreete' by Stow.

ADDLE STREET, WOOD STREET — 3M CE1 BH
Adle St; —; —

ALDERMANBURY — 3N,4N CE1&2 BH
Aldersmā Bury; Ald omanne Bury; —

ALDERMANBURY CONDUIT (W5) — 3N CE1 BH

ALDERMANBURY WELL (W4) — 4M CE2 BH
According to Stow there had been a well here with two buckets which was converted into a pump. The drawing on the maps shows the well. Later called Aldermanbury Pump.

ALDERSGATE (GATE) (G8) — 3L,4L BH
Alders gate; —; Alders Gate

ALDERSGATE STREET — 2L,3L BH
Aldersgate Streate; —; —

ALDGATE BARS — 4V BH
The Barres; —; The Barres
Aldgate Bars, marking the eastern boundary of the City, are not shown in the correct position on either 'Agas' or BH. The wide road running north from Whitechapel Road is almost certainly intended to be Brick Lane. The bars should be situated approximately in the centre of square 4U.

ALDGATE (GATE) (G2) — 4T BH
Alde gate; —; All Gate

ALDGATE HIGH STREET
see: Aldgate (Street)

ALDGATE (STREET) — 4T,4U BH
The part of the street outside the gate is now called Aldgate High Street.

ALDGATE STREET — 4S,4T CE2 BH
The road at present called 'Aldgate' is referred to in this index as 'Aldgate (Street)'.
In Stow's time Aldgate Street included part of what is now called Leadenhall Street, and extended from Lime Street to the Well (W6).

ALDGATE WELL (W6) — 4T BH
From the drawing on the map it would appear to be a well. It was later converted into a pump and is described as such by Stow.

ALL HALLOWS BARKING, AND CHURCHYARD — 6T BH
Barkyng; —; —
'Agas' map letter B, shown reversed.

ALL HALLOWS, BREAD STREET — 5M BH
'Agas' map number 5, shown reversed. In 1559 the stone steeple (shown on 'Agas') was struck by lightning and shortly afterwards taken down.

ALL HALLOWS, HONEY LANE — (4M)
Not shown. It stood close by St. Mary Magdalen, Milk Street (16).

ALL HALLOWS LANE
see: Church Lane, Upper Thames Street.

ALL HALLOWS, LOMBARD STREET, AND CHURCHYARD — 5R CE2 BH
'Agas' map letter H.
The rebuilding of this church was completed in 1544.

ALL HALLOWS, LONDON WALL, AND CHURCHYARD — 3Q CE1 BH
All Holoues in ÿ Wall; All holyes ni the Wall; All holyes ni the Wall
'Agas' map number 28.

Entry	Ref		
ALL HALLOWS STAINING — 'Agas' map letter C, shown reversed.	5S	CE2	BH
ALL HALLOWS THE GREAT, AND CHURCHYARD — 'Agas' map letter V.	6Q	CE2	BH
ALL HALLOWS THE LESS — 'Agas' map letter M.	6Q	CE2	BH
AMEN CORNER	5K		BH
ANDREW COURT	5G		BH
ANDRO MORRIS KEY — Andrew morice kay; —; —	7T		BH
APPOLD STREET	2Q		BH
ARMOURERS' HALL — Surmised from garden shown.	3P	CE1	BH
ARTILLERY YARD	2S	CE1	BH
ARUNDEL HOUSE — Arundel Place; —; Arundell P Arundel House stood to the west of Milford Lane. Formerly the town house of the Bishops of Bath, Arundel House passed into the hands of Lord Thomas Seymour during the reign of Edward VI and was purchased by the Earl of Arundel in 1549.	5F		BH
AUSTIN FRIARS — S. Augusti; Fr. Augustines; — At the Dissolution of the Monasteries, part of the priory of Augustinian Friars was given by the King to Sir Richard Rich, and other parts, including the church, were given to William Paulet who built a large house called Paulet, or Winchester, House (q.v.). In 1550 Edward VI granted the church to the Dutch nation.	4Q	CE2	BH
AVE MARIA LANE — Ave Mari la; —	5K		BH
BAKERS' HALL — Surmised from the garden shown.	6T	CE2	BH
BAKEWELL HALL — Sometimes called Blackwell Hall. Used as a market for woollen cloth in Stow's time.	4N	CE2	BH
BANGOR INN — The London residence of the Bishops of Bangor.	4H		BH
BANK END, SOUTHWARK	7P		BH
BANKSIDE — The Banck; —;	7M		BH
BARBER SURGEONS' HALL (approx. site)	3M		BH
BARBICAN (STREET) — Barbican; —; Barbocan	2L,3L		BH
BARBICAN (TOWER) (X121) — On both the 'Agas' map and BH, the word Barbican appears directly below the tower. It could apply either to the tower or to the street.	2L		BH
BARGE HOUSE STAIRS	7G		BH
BARKLEY'S INN — Originally built by the Lords of Barkley, it was in ruins and let as tenements in Stow's time.	6L		BH
BARNARD'S INN — An Inn of Chancery attached to Grays Inn.	4H		BH
BARTHOLOMEW CLOSE CONDUIT (W19)	3L		BH
BARTHOLOMEW FAIR, SITE OF (X179)	3K		BH
BARTHOLOMEW LANE — Bartelmew la; S. Bart lane; —	4P,4Q	CE2	BH
BASINGHALL STREET — Basyngs Hall; Basinshall; —	3N,4N	CE2	BH
BASING LANE — Basing lane; —; —	5M		BH
BATH INN — Also called Bath Place or Bath House, it belonged to William Bourchier, Earl of Bath (d. 1623). Stow describes it as 'of late for the most part new builded'.	4G		BH
BATTLE BRIDGE, TOOLEY STREET — Battle bridge; —; Battle braloe Name derived from the nearby Inn of the Abbots of Battle Abbey, Sussex, which stood here up to the time the map was compiled.	8U		BH
BAYNARD'S CASTLE — Baynardes Castel; —; Benan's Castle Constructed in 1275 on newly reclaimed land, after the building of Blackfriars Priory enclosed the former Norman castle erected by Ralph Baynard.	6K		BH
BEARBINDER LANE — Bearebȳder la; —;	5P,5Q	CE2	BH
BEAR GARDEN, SOUTHWARK — The Beare bayting; —; The Beare bayting The 'Agas' map only shows the back of an animal in the ring but BH, although so small, clearly shows a bear sitting up being attacked by a dog.	8N		BH
BEDFORD HOUSE — Originally called Carlisle Inn after its owner the Bishop of Carlisle. It was obtained by Lord Russell in 1539. He was created Earl of Bedford in 1550.	5D		BH
BEECH LANE — Bech la; —; Now called Beech Street.	2M		BH

BEER HOUSE NO. 1 (X110)
Beere howse; —; Beere howse
Records of Horsleydown describe a Sir John Fastolfe as owning four messuages called beer houses here. The site is probably beside what later maps (both Morgan and Rocque) call Pickle Herring Stairs.
8V BH

BEER HOUSE NO. 2
—; —; Beere howse
This building is too far E. to be shown on 'Agas'. It is E. of map location 6W and it is possible that before they were damaged the original 'Agas' wood blocks extended this far.
BH

BEER HOUSE NO. 3 (X119)
—; —; Beere howse
5C CE1 BH

BEER LANE
Burre la; —; —
6T BH

BELL YARD
5G BH

BENBRIDGE INN
Mentioned by Stow as being on the N.W. corner of Lime Street.
4R CE2 BH

BENNET'S HILL
see: Paul's Chaine
4S CE2 BH

BEREWARDS LANE
see: Hog Lane, Portsoken
Led from Bishopsgate to Hog Lane (or Petticoat Lane) and was later called Hog Lane.
4S,5S CE2 BH

BERMONDSEY STREET
Kent str; —; Barne strete
The 'Agas' map seems confused in the naming of Tooley Street (q.v.), which is called 'Barms strete', and Bermondsey Street which is called 'Kent str'. The Old Kent Road used to be called Kent Street but lies too far S. to be shown on 'Agas'. A map of Horsleydown dated 1544
8U,8V BH

shows Bermondsey Street, which led to Bermondsey Abbey, as 'Barmondsey Street'. It seems that 'Barms strete' (shown in the wrong place on 'Agas') should therefore have represented Bermondsey Street.

BETHLEHEM HOSPITAL
Bedlem gate; Bedlame Gate, Bedlame; Berlame
In 1547 Henry VIII gave the building of the dissolved Priory of Canons, with brethren & sisters, of the Order of St. Mary of Bethlehem, to the City of London for conversion into a lunatic asylum.
3R CE1 BH

BETHLEHEM HOSPITAL CHAPEL (X145)
3R CE1 BH

BEVIS MARKS (HOUSE) (approx. site)
Once the London house of the Abbots of Bury St. Edmunds. Called Heneage House after the owner Sir Thomas who was granted the property in 1540.
4S CE2 BH

BEVIS MARKS (STREET)
4S CE2 BH

BILLINGSGATE
Bylynges gate; —; Belins Gate
London's principal dock in Stow's time.
7S CE2 BH

BILLITER LANE
Bylleter la; Belliter lane; —
Now called Billiter Street.
4S,5S CE2 BH

BIRCHIN LANE
Burchin; —; —
Stow refers to it as 'Birchovers lane'.
5Q CE2 BH

BISHOPSGATE (GATE) (G3)
Busshoppes Gate; BVSSHOPPES GATE; Busshoppes Gate
On CE1 the quarters and limbs of
3R CE1 BH

convicted traitors can be seen impaled on poles.

BISHOPSGATE (STREET)
Busshoppes gate strete, Busshopp gate streate; Busshoppes gate Strete, Byshopps gate strete; Busshoppes gate Strete.
In each case the first spelling is for the street beyond the gate. On CE1 a well and a cross are drawn just S. of Hog Lane; they do not appear on the other two maps.
2R-4R CE1&2 BH

BISHOPSGATE WELL, WITHIN (W11)
It had been converted into a pump when Stow wrote.
4R CE2 BH

BISHOPSGATE WELL, WITHOUT (W10)
It later became a pump.
2R CE1 BH

BLACKFRIARS
Formerly a house of Dominican Friars, it was surrendered to Henry VIII and the site given to Thomas Cawardine in 1549-50.
5K,6K BH

BLACK HOUSE (X122)
—; Blak hows; —
This name appears only on CE, but the house is shown on all three maps.
3R CE1 BH

BLACKSMITHS' HALL (approx. site)
6L BH

BLACKWELL HALL
see: Bakewell Hall
4L BH

BLADDER STREET
5S CE2 BH

BLANCH APPLETON
Blanck chapelton; Blächapelton; —
It is variously described as a manor or a messuage.
5S CE2 BH

BLOSSOM INN, ST. LAWRENCE LANE (approx. site)
4N CE2 BH

BOROUGH HIGH STREET
see: Long Southwark

BOSS ALLEY — 6L — BH
Boss allee; —; —

BOTOLPH LANE — 6R — CE2 — BH
Butolphe lane; Butow lane; —

BOTOLPH'S WHARF — 7R — CE2 — BH
Buttolphe W; —; Botoll wharff

BOW LANE — 4N,5N — CE2 — BH
Bowe lane; Buo lane; —
The name 'Buo lane' appears twice on CE2, once here and again further S. on the same street which is better known now as Garlick Hill (q.v.). Stow calls it 'Cordwainer street corruptly called Bow Lane'. Another reference in Harben calls it 'Hosier Lane alias Bow Lane'. Its earlier names were probably Hosier Lane at the N. end and Cordwainer Street further S.

BOWYER ROW — 5K — BH

BOWYERS' HALL (approx. site) — 3M — BH

BREAD STREET — 4M,5M — BH
Bread streat; —; —

BREAD STREET HILL — 6M — BH
Bread Streat; —; —

BREWERS' HALL (approx. site) — 3M — BH

BRICK LANE — 2V-4V — BH
If the mapmakers intended this to be Brick Lane then Aldgate Bars should be in the centre of grid reference 4U.

BRICKLAYERS' HALL (approx. site) — 4S — CE2 — BH

BRIDE LANE — 5J — BH

BRIDEWELL — 6J — BH
Bride Well; —; Bridwell
Built as a palace for Henry VIII, 1515-23. Presented to the City of London by Edward VI as a work-house for the poor and a House of Correction.

BRIDEWELL BRIDGE — 5J — BH
Built 1522.

BRIDGE HOUSE — 8S — BH
The bridge howse; —; —
From here, wardens appointed by the City collected the revenue derived from leases, house rents, tolls, etc., for the upkeep of London Bridge. Corn and materials for repairing the bridge were kept in nearby storehouses.

BROAD STREET — 4Q — CE1&2 — BH
Brode streat; Brodd strete; —
Now called 'Old Broad Street'.

BROADWALL — 7G,8G — BH
This was an ancient dyke running between ditches draining the Lambeth marsh. The path at the southern end was called Angel Street. The name appears on both Morgan's and Rocque's maps.

BROKEN WHARF — 6M — BH
Broken Wharfe; —; Braken warf
Stow refers to 'one large old building of stone with arched gates' by Broken Wharf, and calls it Bygots House. This had formerly been in the possession of the Dukes of Norfolk. It appears to be shown on BH but not 'Agas'.

BUCKLERSBURY — 5P — CE2 — BH
Buclersbury; Bookelers bury; —
See also X150.

BUDGE ROW — 5P — CE2 — BH
Budge rowe; Bougge Row; —

BULL BAITING, SOUTHWARK — 8M — BH
The bolle bayting; —; The Bowll bayting
Both 'Agas' and BH show a bull and a dog in the ring.

BUNHILL FIELD — 1M,1N — CE1 — BH
A little difficult to place on the 'Agas' map. The Field lay N.W. of the windmills and W. of the lane which ran due N. from Moorgate. Part of this lane is shown on CE1 running N. on the W. side of windmill (X8). See also Finsbury Court.

BURLEY HOUSE — 6L — BH

BURY STREET — 4S — CE2 — BH

BUSH LANE — 6Q — CE2 — BH
Bush lane; Buche lane; —

BUTCHERS' HALL (approx. site) — 4L — BH
Their hall was in Monkwell Street until 1548 when a new hall was built in St. Nicholas Shambles.

BUTCHER ROW — 5F,5G — BH

CAMOMILE STREET — 3R,4R — CE2 — BH

CANDLEWICK STREET — 5P,5Q — CE2 — BH
Canwicke str; Canon strete; —
Note that at the time of the map Candlewick Street, which was later called Cannon Street, only extended west to the junction with Walbrook. However, its line when extended in 1854 took in: Maiden Lane, Pissing Lane, Basing Lane, Little St. Thomas Apostles, Turnbase Lane and Budge Row.

CANNON ROW, WESTMINSTER — 7B — BH
Chanoi row; —; Chanoy Row
Houses for the Dean and Canons of St. Stephen's were built here in the reign of Henry VI. Afterwards

its nearness to Court made it a favourite place for the residence of noblemen and gentlemen.

CANNON STREET see: Candlewick Street.

CAREY LANE Kerie la; —; — Called 'Kery Lane' by Stow. — 4M BH

CARPENTERS' HALL (approx. site) — 3P CE1

CARTER LANE Carter lane; —; — — 5K,5L BH

CASTELL UPON THE HOPE INN (X216) One of the Southwark stewhouses (i.e. a brothel). Referred to in 1559 as the 'Castell on the hoope'. Later the site of the Anchor public house. — 8P BH

CASTLE ALLEY Castel hill; —; — — 6L BH

CATEATON STREET Keton st; —; — Known also as 'Catte Street' and 'Catteton Street', it now forms part of Gresham Street. — 4N CE2 BH

CHANCERY LANE Chancerie la; —; — Stow says it was called 'New Street' or Chancelar lane'. — 4G,5G BH

CHARING CROSS Charing crosse; —; Charyncros One of the 12 memorial crosses erected by Edward I to mark the stages in the funeral procession of his queen, Eleanor. See also Eleanor Cross, Cheapside (X13). A gallows is shown just S. of the cross on BH. — 5B BH

CHARTERHOUSE Charterhouse; —; Charterhowse Formerly a monastery of Carthusian monks, it was sold in 1544 to Sir Edward North who converted it into a town-house. On BH the church is seen standing free and complete, with a central spire, but this appears to have been replaced by a long low building on 'Agas'—possibly North's Great Hall, but more probably the church.

CHARTERHOUSE LANE Charterhouse lane; —; — — 3K BH

CHEAPSIDE Chepesyde; —; — The earlier names were 'Cheap' (meaning 'a market') or 'Westcheap' to distinguish it from Eastcheap, at the eastern end of the City. — 4L-4N CE2 BH

CHERTSEY HOUSE Stow says it was called Sandie House in his time. It formerly belonged to the Abbots of Chertsey. — 6L BH

CHICK LANE, SMITHFIELD Called 'Chicken Lane' by Stow. — 3J BH

CHICK LANE, TOWER WARD — 6T BH

CHISWELL STREET Chiswell str; —; — The name was in use from at least the 1550s. Stow refers to the street as 'Everardeswellestrete'. — 2M,2N BH

CHRIST CHURCH, NEWGATE STREET In 1547 the church of the Greyfriars became the parish church of Christ within Newgate. — 4K BH

CHRIST CHURCH PRIORY see: Holy Trinity Priory

CHRIST'S HOSPITAL Founded 1552. The buildings of the former Greyfriars monastery were repaired and furnished for the maintenance of poor fatherless children.

CHRIST'S HOSPITAL POSTERN (G8a) — 4K BH

CHURCH ALLEY — 3N CE2 BH

CHURCH LANE, UPPER THAMES STREET Church la; —; — Later known as All Hallows Lane. — 6Q CE2 BH

CITY DITCH It extended almost completely around the City, outside the wall. It was referred to also as 'Houndsditch' (q.v.), hence the street of this name sometimes just 'the Ditch'. By the 16th century most of it had been built over as gardens on the W. side of the City, less so on the E. side. — 4K,3L-3S,4S,4T CE1&2 BH

CITY DOG HOUSE Dogge house; Dogge hows; — This was moved to the N. side of Finsbury Field in 1570. — 3Q CE1 BH

CITY WALL For a list of gates and bastions see under the sections so named. One topographical error shown on both the 'Agas' map and BH is that when extrapolated southwards from Aldgate, the City Wall aligns with a point some distance W. of the White Tower. Its true line ran just E. of the White Tower. — 5J,5K, 4K,4L, 3L-3S, 4S,4T CE1&2 BH

CLEMENT'S INN An Inn of Chancery appertaining to the Inner Temple. — 4G BH

CLEMENT'S LANE see: St. Clement's Lane

Entry	Ref		
CLERKENWELL Clarken Well; —; Clarkenwell	2J		BH
CLERKENWELL GREEN	2J		BH
CLERKENWELL ROAD	2H,2J		BH
CLERK'S WELL (W3)	2H		BH
CLIFFORD'S INN (approx. site) An Inn of Chancery appertaining to the Inner Temple.	5H		BH
CLINK PRISON (approx. site)	8P		BH
CLINK STREET	8P		BH
CLOAK LANE Stow calls it 'Horsebridge Street' in one place and 'Horseshoe Bridge Street' in another.	5N,6N, 6P	CE2	BH
CLOCK TOWER, WESTMINSTER 'Agas' map letter A. It stood on the N. boundary of the land belonging to the Palace of Westminster.	7A		BH
CLOTHWORKERS' HALL (approx. site)	5S	CE2	BH
COCK LANE Cocke l; —; —	4J		BH
[COCKSPUR STREET]	4A,4B, 5B		BH
COLDHARBOUR —; Showsbury P; Showsburÿ P Given the name of its owner by CE and BH. This large messuage was granted to the Earl of Shrewsbury in 1553, who leased the eastern portion to the Watermen's Company for their Hall with the quays and watergate.	6Q	CE2	BH
COLEMAN STREET Colman street; Colmans strete; —	3N,4P	CE1&2	BH
COLEMAN STREET CONDUIT Stow says 'by the west end of this parish church (St. Margaret,	(4P)	CE2	

Entry	Ref		
Lothbury) have ye a fair water conduit'. Erected in 1546.			
COLLEGE HILL Whytyngton Colleage; Winthm. College; — It is uncertain whether 'Whytyngton Colleage' refers to the street or the college (q.v.)	6N	CE2	BH
COLLEGE OF ARMS (approx. site)	5L		BH
CONVENT GARDEN The Convent garden (later 'Covent Garden') was acquired by Henry VIII in 1536 from Westminster Abbey and used as pasture for sheep. It was later granted to Protector Somerset and in 1552 it was owned by John Russell, first Earl of Bedford.	4C-4E		BH
COOKS' HALL Surmised from garden shown.	3L		BH
COOPERS' HALL Surmised from garden shown.	4N	CE2	BH
COOPERS ROW see: Woodroffe Lane			
COPE KEY —; Cope kay	(6R)		BH
CORDWAINERS' HALL (approx. site)	5M		BH
CORNHILL —; CORNWELL; —	4Q,4R	CE2	BH
CORNHILL STREET It should not be confused with Cornhill. Today Cornhill Street is the part of Leadenhall Street between Gracechurch Street and Lime Street.	4R	CE2	BH
CORNHILL TUN A conduit, so called because it looked like a barrel. Water jugs are shown beside it.	(4Q)	CE2	BH

Entry	Ref		
CORNHILL WELL Later became a conduit; Stow calls it the 'Little Conduit'.	(4Q)	CE2	BH
COURT GATE, WHITEHALL The Courte gate; —; —	6B		BH
COUSIN LANE	6P	CE2	BH
COVENT GARDEN see: Convent Garden			
COW BRIDGE, SMITHFIELD	3J		BH
COW CROSS STREET Cowe crosse; —; —	3J		BH
COW LANE Cowe la; —; — Also called Smithfield Street.	3J,4J		BH
CREECHURCH LANE	4S	CE2	BH
CREED LANE Crede la; —; —	5K		BH
CRIPPLEGATE (G6) Creplegate; —; Cripil Gate	3M		BH
CRIPPLEGATE CONDUIT, WITHOUT (W14) Water-vessels are shown beside it on BH.	3M		BH
CROCKERS LANE	5H		BH
CROMWELL HOUSE see: Drapers' Hall			
CROOKED LANE Croked la; Crouked lane; —	6Q,6R	CE2	BH
CROSBY HALL Built in the mid-15th century by Sir John Crosby. The hall has now been removed to Chelsea.	4R	CE2	BH
CRUTCHED FRIARS (PRIORY) The priory was surrendered in 1538. Many of the buildings remained and the friar's house was used as a glass factory.	5T		BH

CRUTCHED FRIARS (STREET) 5T BH
At the time of the map Crutched Friars seems to have run N.E. from the well (W7) whereas today Crutched Friars starts from the junction with Seething Lane.

CURRIERS' HALL (approx. site) 3M BH

CURRIERS ROW 3P CE1 BH

[CURTAIN ROAD] 2Q

CUSTOM HOUSE 7T BH
Costume house; —; Castum howse

CUTLERS' HALL (approx. site) 6N CE2 BH

DEAD MAN'S PLACE 8P BH
So called on both Morgan and Rocque. Park Street now follows the line of this path. A little more of this street can be seen on BH.

DISTAFF LANE 5M BH
Distaf la; —; —

DOCTORS' COMMONS (approx. site) 5L BH
It stood on the S. side of Knightrider Street, W. of Paul's Chaine. A college of doctors of law.

DO LITTLE LANE 5L
Do lytle la; —; —

DOLPHIN INN, BISHOPSGATE 3R CE1 BH
'A common Inne for receipt of travellers' (Stow).

DOWGATE (HILL) 6P CE2 BH
Dowe gate; Doo gate; —

DRAPERS' ALMSHOUSES 2M BH

DRAPERS' HALL 4Q CE2 BH
The hall had been built for Thomas Cromwell and was known as Cromwell House. It was acquired by the Drapers' Company in 1541.

DREWRY HOUSE 2M BH
Previously used as the town house of the Abbot of Ramsey and called an Inn.

DRURY HOUSE 4F BH
Shown and named on both Norden and Morgan.

DRURY LANE 3D,3E, 4E BH

DUCKSFOOT LANE
see: St. Laurence Lane.

DURHAM HOUSE 5D BH
Duresme Pl; —; Duresme P
The London house of the Bishops of Durham. Queen Elizabeth I granted it to Sir Henry Sidney.

DYERS' HALL (approx. site) 6Q CE2 BH
In the late 15th century the hall had been in Anchor Lane, just W. of Vintners Hall.The company moved at some time between that date and the late 16th century.

EASTCHEAP 6R CE2 BH
Eschepe; Excheapp; —
At the time of these maps Eastcheap ran from St. Martin's Lane to Tower Street (now Great Tower Street). The section W. of New Fish Street was known also as 'Great Eastcheap', the eastern part being 'Little Eastcheap' (q.v.).

EAST SMITHFIELD 5W BH
Easte smith; —; —
This area was called 'East Smithfield' to distinguish it from the Smithfield on the west side of the City. Comparison of the three extant 'Agas' maps shows that the full name did originally appear as 'Easte smithfelt'.

ELEANOR CROSS, CHEAPSIDE (X13) 4M BH
One of 12 memorial crosses erected by Edward I to mark the stages in the funeral procession of his queen, Eleanor. See also Charing Cross.

ELY PLACE 4H BH
Ely place; —; —
The London house of the Bishops of Ely. It was occasionally let by the see to distinguished noblemen.

ELY PLACE GARDEN 3H,4H BH

EMBROIDERERS' HALL (approx. site) 4M BH

ERBER, THE (approx. site) 6P CE2 BH
A mansion on the E. side of Dowgate.

FALCON INN, SOUTHWARK 7J BH

FALCON STAIRS 7K BH

FARRINGDON ROAD 2H BH

FENCHURCH STREET 4T, 5R-5T CE2 BH

FENCHURCH STREET WELL (W8) 5S CE2
Not mentioned by Stow or Harben.

FETTER LANE 4H,5H BH
Fetter lane; —; —
Called 'Fewtars lane' by Stow.

FINCH LANE 4Q CE2 BH
Finke la; Fynges l; —

FINSBURY COURT 2N CE1 BH
Finsburie Co; Fynnesb Courte; —
This was the manor farm of Finsbury Manor. There were three large fields: Finsbury Field, Mallow Field and Bunhill Field.

Entry	Ref	Code	Source
FINSBURY FIELD Fynesburie Fyeld; FYNNESBVRIE FIELD; — The name is on the E. side of the road leading from Finsbury Court on the 'Agas' map and on the W. side on the CE. The CE is correct and the 'Agas' map has confused Finsbury Field with Mallow Field. Finsbury Field was also known as High Field. See also Finsbury Court.	2N,2P	CE1	BH
FISHER'S FOLLY Elaborate buildings built by Jasper Fisher, a Chancery clerk of no great status.	3R	CE1	BH
FISHMONGERS' HALL	6R	CE2	BH
FISH STREET HILL see: New Fish Street			
FISH WHARF	7R	CE2	BH
FLEET BRIDGE Fleete bruge; —; —	5J		BH
FLEET DITCH A common name for the River Fleet (q.v.).			
FLEET LANE Flete, Fleete la; —; — In Stow's time the eastern end out of Old Bailey to Seacole Lane was called 'St. George's Lane'.	4J,5J, 4K		BH
FLEET PRISON (approx. site)	4J		BH
FLEET, RIVER Farringdon Street now follows the course of this stream. See also Fleet Ditch and Turnmill Brook.	2H,3H, 4J-6J		BH
FLEET STREET Fleete streate; —; —	5G-5J		BH
FLEET STREET CONDUIT (W9) Rebuilt 1582. BH shows water-vessels beside the conduit.	5H		BH

Entry	Ref	Code	Source
FLETCHERS' HALL Surmised from garden shown.	4S		BH
FORE STREET Fore str; —; — According to Stow the eastern part of this street was called 'Postern Lane', because 'it hath at eyther end a doore to be shut in the night season'. These two doors or gates appear on the map (X76 & X77) roughly drawn. They are more accurately drawn on CE1.	3M-3P	CE1	BH
FOSTER LANE Forster lane; —; —	4L		BH
FOUNDERS' HALL (approx. site) Stow says it stood beside the W. side of the church of St. Margaret, Lothbury.	4P	CE2	BH
FOUR CORNERS —; 4 Canti; — The cross roads referred to by Stow where Lombard Street and Fenchurch Street meet Grace-church Street is clearly named on CE2 in Italian.	5R	CE2	BH
FOWLE LANE Now called St. Dunstan's Lane.	6S	CE2	BH
FRESH WHARF Freshe W; Freshe; Freshe warf It was made a general place for loading and discharging goods by Act of Parliament, 1559.	6R	CE1	BH
FRIDAY STREET Fryda streat; —; —	4M,5M		BH
FURNIVAL'S INN An Inn of Chancery attached to Lincoln's Inn.	4H		BH
GALLEY KEY —; —; Gallÿ k	7T		BH

Entry	Ref	Code	Source
GARLICK HILL Garl hyll; Buo lane; — The name 'Buo lane' appears twice on CE2, indicating that Bow Lane may have once extended S. to include what is now Garlick Hill.	6N	CE2	BH
GARTER HOUSE	2L		BH
GAYSPUR LANE It was renamed 'Aldermanbury' after about 1750.	3N	CE1	BH
GEORGE YARD	6L		BH
GERRARDS HALL (approx. site) 'Now a common hostelry for receipt of travellers' (Stow).	5M		BH
GIARDIN DI PIERO (X123) —; Giardin di Piero; — Peter's Garden is not mentioned by Stow. Martin Holmes has suggested that it may have been used for bear-baiting.	3R	CE1	BH
GILTSPUR STREET Gilford st; —; —	4K		BH
GIRDLERS' HALL Surmised from garden shown.	3N	CE1	BH
GLAZIERS' HALL (approx. site) It stood in Kerion Lane (q.v.), just N. of St. Martin Vintry church.	6N	CE2	BH
GODLIMAN STREET see: Paul's Chaine			
GOLDEN LANE Golding lane; —; — The cross (X43) shown at the N. end of Whitecross Street should probably be at the N. end of Golden Lane.	2L		BH
GOLDSMITHS' HALL (approx. site)	4M		BH
GOODMANS FIELDS	4U,4V		BH

GOSWELL ROAD 1K,2K BH
The Waye to S. Alban; —; — Stow calls it 'Goswel streete'.

GRACECHURCH STREET 5R CE1 BH
Gracyons streate; Grachios strete; —

GRACECHURCH STREET CONDUIT (5R) CE2 BH

GRAVEL LANE 8H,8J BH

GRAYS INN 3G BH
An Inn of Court, established for the study and practice of law, with two Inns of Chancery attached (Staple Inn and Barnard's Inn; q.v.).

GRAYS INN ROAD 2G-4G BH
Greys ynne la; —; — Called 'Porte Poole or Grayes Inne lane' according to Stow.

GREAT CONDUIT, CHEAPSIDE (W17) 4N,5N CE2 BH

GREAT DISTAFF LANE
see: Maiden Lane, Friday Street

GREAT ST. THOMAS APOSTLE (STREET) 5N BH
The name 'S. Thomas Apostel' in this street may refer to the church of St. Thomas Apostle (q.v.).

GREAT TOWER HILL
see: Tower Hill

GREAT TOWER STREET
see: Tower Street

GREAT TRINITY LANE
see: Old Fish Street

GRESHAM HOUSE 4Q,4R CE2 BH
The mansion of Sir Thomas Gresham. After his death in 1579 it became Gresham College, London's first centre of higher education.

GRESHAM STREET
see: St. Anne's Lane
　　Maiden Lane, Wood Street
　　Lad Lane
　　Cateaton Street
The following streets (in order W. to E.) were amalgamated and called Gresham Street in 1877: St. Anne's Lane, Maiden Lane, Lad Lane, Cateaton Street.

GREY FRIARS 4K BH
Gray Fryers; —; — The name is shown on the City Wall. A house of Franciscan Friars, surrendered in 1538. The Grey Friars' church became Christ Church (q.v.) in 1547. See also Christ's Hospital.

GROCERS' HALL 4P CE2 BH
The hall itself is not discernible on 'Agas' but is clearly shown on CE2. The large garden and tower X199 are part of the hall.

GRUB STREET 2M BH
Grub str; —; — Called Milton St. since 1830.

GUILDHALL 4N CE2 BH
Gulde hall; Guylthe hall; —

GUILDHALL CHAPEL 4N BH
Known as the Chapel of St. Mary Magdalen.

GULLY HOLE, TOOLEY STREET 8T BH
Named as such on Morgan's and Rocque's map.

GUNFOUNDRY, HOUNDSDITCH 4T BH
—; —; Ye Goounefowuders hs

GUTTER LANE 4M BH
Goutter lane; —; — Called 'Guthron's Lane' by Stow.

HABERDASHERS' HALL (approx. site) 4M BH

HANGING SWORD COURT 5H BH

HARP LANE 6S CE2 BH
Harpe lane; harpe lane; — Also known as 'Hart Lane'.

HART STREET 5T CE2 BH
Herte str; —; — At time of the map Hart Street seems to have extended from Mark Lane to Woodroffe Lane. The eastern half is now called Crutched Friars.

HART STREET WELL (W7) 5T BH
Neither Stow nor Harben refers to a well here.

HAYMARKET 4A BH
Vertue has written Haymarket on his copy of the map.

HAYWHARF 6Q CE2 BH

HEDGE LANE 4B BH

HENEAGE HOUSE
see: Bevis Marks (House)

HIGH HOLBORN 3E,3F,4G BH
Stow speaks of 'high Oldborne street'.

HOCKLEY IN THE HOLE 2G,2H BH

HOG LANE, EAST SMITHFIELD 5W BH
Hogge la; —; — Called 'Hog Street' by Stow. It is now called 'Royal Mint Street'.

HOG LANE, NORTON FOLGATE 8T BH
Later called Worship Street.

HOG LANE, PORTSOKEN 2P-2R CE1 BH; 2R,3S CE1 BH
A deed of 1607 refers to it as 'Petticoat Lane', a name still in use today. Its official modern name is Middlesex Street. The top end was also known as 'Berewards Lane' or 'Berwards Lane'.

Entry	Grid	Source	Source
HOLBORN Houlburne; —; Howlburne To the W. of the junction with Chancery Lane the road is called High Holborn (q.v.).	4G,4H		BH
HOLBORN BARS The bares; —; — The western boundary of the City of London.	4G		BH
HOLBORN BRIDGE Holburne bridge; —; —	4J		BH
HOLBORN CONDUIT (W15)	4J		BH
HOLBORN HILL	4J		BH
HOLBORN MANOR Also known as Holborn Hall.	4J		BH
HOLY TRINITY CHAPEL, LEADENHALL see: Leadenhall Chapel			
HOLY TRINITY, MINORIES Not shown. This had previously been the church of the Abbey of St. Clare (q.v.), surrendered 1538. It was situated at the N.W. corner of Goodmans Fields.	(4U)		BH
HOLY TRINITY PRIORY Cry chur; CRY CHURCHE; — The priory was dissolved in 1531. It was later pulled down and a house built on the site (afterwards called Duke's Place).	4S,4T	CE2	BH
HOLY TRINITY THE LESS Not shown. It stood at N. end of Trinity Lane on the E. side.	(5M)		BH
HOLYWELL STREET, STRAND	5F		BH
HORSLEYDOWN Horssey downe; —; —	8W		BH
HOSIER LANE Hosyer l; —; —	3J,4J		BH
HOUNDSDITCH Honnsdiche; VNDICHE; —	3R,3S, 4T	CE1	BH
HUGGIN LANE, THAMES STREET Huggyng lane; —; — Now called Huggin Hill.	5M,6M		BH
HUGGIN LANE, WOOD STREET Hoggyn la; —; — Written 'Huggen Lane' by Stow.	4M		BH
HUNGERFORD HOUSE A large house with grounds extending to the river, owned by the Hungerford family.	5C		BH
IDOL LANE see: St. Dunstan's Hill.	5G		BH
INNER TEMPLE An Inn of Court, established for the study and practice of the law. See also under Temple.	5G		BH
INNHOLDERS' HALL Surmised from garden shown.	6P	CE2	BH
IRON GATE STAIRS	6W		BH
IRONMONGER LANE Iremonger lane; Earmonger l; —	4N	CE2	BH
IRONMONGERS' HALL (approx. site)	5S	CE2	BH
ISLINGTON	1J,1K		BH
IVY BRIDGE LANE, STRAND Yuie brydge; —; —	5D		BH
IVY LANE, PATERNOSTER ROW Yuie la; —; —	4L		BH
JEWRY STREET see: Poor Jewry			
JOINERS' HALL (approx. site)	6P	CE2	BH
KERION LANE It ran N. out of Thames Street, then E. behind St. Martin Vintry. Later known as 'Maiden Lane'. The entrance in Thames Street is just visible on 'Agas', CE2 and BH.	6N	CE2	BH
KETTON STREET see: Cateaton Street			
KING STREET, WESTMINSTER Kinges streate; —; — Now called Parliament St. and Whitehall.	5B,6B, 6A,7A		BH
KING'S WARDROBE The wardrop; —; — The office of the Master of the Wardrobe and the repository for the royal clothes.	5K		BH
KNIGHTRIDER STREET Knyght streat; —; —	5L		BH
LAD LANE Lad la; —; — Renamed Gresham Street in 1845.	4M		BH
LAMBETH The lambeht; —; Lamberth The BH map, although smaller, is more accurate topographically than 'Agas' here. On the 'Agas' map, Lambeth Palace is almost due E. of Westminster Abbey. In fact Lambeth Palace is much further S. and is so drawn on BH.	8C		BH
LAMBETH HILL, THAMES STREET Lambert hyll; —; —	5L,6L		BH
LAMBETH MARSH —; —; Lamberth Marche	7C		BH
LAMBETH PALACE see also: Lambeth	8C		BH
[LAMBETH ROAD]	8C		BH
LAMBETH STAIRS This was also the site of a horse ferry. Although BH appears to be drawn	8B		BH

43

more accurately than 'Agas', the landing stage on the Westminster bank is not shown on BH. On the W. bank the road leading to the ferry acquired the name of Horse-ferry Road.

LAMB'S CONDUIT
see: Holborn Conduit

LAURENCE POUNTNEY HILL
see: St. Laurence Pountney Hill

LAURENCE POUNTNEY LANE
see: St. Laurence Hill, Thames Street

LAWRENCE LANE
see: St. Laurence Lane, Guildhall — 4R,5R — CE2 — BH

LEADENHALL
Leaden hall; Ledden hall; — A large mansion, converted into a granary and market in the late medieval period. Scales for weighing meal (mentioned in Stow) appear on all 3 maps. The chapel (X200) is also visible. — BH

[LEADENHALL STREET]
Known as 'Aldgate Street' and 'Cornhill Street' at the time of the 'Agas' map. The earliest reference found is 'Leaden Hall Street', 1605. (The present day name is also given on the map to avoid confusion.) Stow sometimes refers to it simply as 'the High Street'. — 4R-4T — CE2 — BH

LEATHER LANE
Liver la; —; Called 'Lither lane' by Stow. — 3H,4H — BH

LEATHERSELLERS' HALL
The site was purchased 1543. It had been part of the Priory of St. Helen. — 4R — CE2 — BH

LEWES INN
Once owned by the Prior of Lewes, it had become a hostelry for travellers in Stow's day. See also: St. Thomas' Hospital. — 8S — BH

LIME STREET
Lyme str; Lyme strete; — — 4S,5S — CE2 — BH

LINCOLN'S INN
An Inn of Court with two Inn's of Chancery attached (Furnival's Inn and Thavies Inn; q.v.). — 4G — BH

[LINCOLN'S INN FIELDS]
In the reign of Elizabeth this was an open waste traversed by ditches and sewers, the haunt of beggars, and the occasional scene of military exercises and public executions. — 4F — BH

LITTLE BAILEY — 4K — BH

LITTLE BRITAIN
Litle Britaine; —; Stow calls it 'Briton stret'. — 3K,3L — BH

LITTLE CONDUIT, CHEAPSIDE (W1) — 4L

LITTLE DRURY LANE — 4F,5F

LITTLE EASTCHEAP — 6R — BH

LITTLE FRIDAY STREET
see: Pissing Alley

LITTLE MOORFIELDS
The name given here is that shown on Morgan's map. Today this street is called 'Moorgate'. — 3P — BH

LITTLE ST. THOMAS APOSTLES (STREET)
S. Thomas lane; —; Stow seems to include this street with Turnbase Lane. There is little evidence for the 'Agas' name being in common usage. This street was — 5N — BH

incorporated into the western extension of Cannon Street in 1854.

LITTLE TOWER HILL — 5V — BH

LITTLE TRINITY LANE
see: Trinity Lane

LITTLE WOOD STREET
Lytil Wood str; —; Now called Wood Street. — 3M — BH

LOMBARD STREET
Lombard street; Lombarde strete; — — 5Q,5R — CE2 — BH

LONDON BRIDGE
London bridge; —; The bridge rested on 19 'starlings' or islands set into the river bed. The 'Agas' map shows 21 starlings, BH shows 20. The ornate structure at the south end of the bridge—usually assumed to be the Great Stone Gate—is in fact meant to represent the elaborate building on the next pier north of the gate. In order not to mask this building the artist has flattened the Great Stone Gate which can be seen in front of it. The chapel of St. Thomas, which had been converted into a house and shop in 1553, is not discernible. — 7R — CE2 — BH

LONDON STONE
London ston; london Stone; — This ancient stone block stood on the S. side of the road opposite St. Swithin's church. Stow describes it in detail. — 5P — CE2 — BH

LONDON WALL
This street ran inside the wall of the City from the N. end of Broad Street (now called Old Broad Street) to Cripplegate. — 3M-3Q — CE1 — BH

LONDON WALL CONDUIT (W18)
Erected in 1517. — 3N — CE1 — BH

Entry	Grid ref		
LONG ACRE This name applied to the large field N. of the Convent Garden. It has now given its name to a street in this area.	3C,4C, 3D,4D		BH
LONG LANE, SMITHFIELD Long Lane; —; —	3K,3L		BH
LONG SOUTHWARK The road is now called the 'Borough High Street'.	8R		BH
LOTHBURY Lothbur; Lothe bury; —	4P	CE2	BH
LOVAT LANE see: Love Lane, Thames Street			
LOVE LANE, THAMES STREET Loue la; loue l; — Called 'Lucas Lane' by Stow, it is called 'Lovat Lane' now.	6S	CE2	BH
LOVE LANE, WOOD STREET Lone la	3M		BH
LOWER THAMES STREET see: Thames Street			
LUDGATE (GATE) (G10) lud gat; —; —	5K		BH
LUDGATE HILL Flete hyll; —; — Only referred to as 'Ludgate Hill' by Stow.	5J,5K		BH
LUMLEY HOUSE Lord Lumley's House, built in Henry VIII's time according to Stow.	5T		BH
LYON KEY Lyon kay; —; Lions k	7R	CE2	BH
LYON'S INN, STRAND An Inn of Chancery belonging to the Inner Temple.	4F,5F		BH
MAIDENHEAD LANE see: Maiden Lane, Friday Street			
MAIDEN LANE, FRIDAY STREET Maidenhead lane; —; — According to Stow 'In this Fryday streete on the west side thereof is a Lane commonly called Mayden Lane or Distaffe Lane, corruptly for Distar lane'.	5M		BH
MAIDEN LANE, WOOD STREET Mayden st; —; — Now called Gresham Street.	4M		BH
MALLOW FIELD Named 'Fynesburie Fyeld' on the 'Agas' map in error. The CE is labelled correctly. See also Finsbury Court.	2P	CE1	BH
MARK LANE Marck lane; Marke lane; —	5S,5T	CE2	BH
MARTIN LANE see: St. Martin's Lane			
MASONS' HALL Surmised from garden shown.	4N	CE2	BH
MAZE, MANOR OF THE	8T		BH
MERCERS' HALL —; S. Tomas; — The collegiate church and hospital of St. Thomas of Acon was surrendered in 1539. The site was purchased by the Mercers who erected a Hall and Chapel on the site. The name on CE2 recalls the old building here.	4N	CE2	BH
MERCHANT TAYLORS' HALL (approx. site)	4Q	CE2	BH
MERCHANT TAYLORS' SCHOOL see: Rose, Manor of			
MIDDLE ROW, HOLBORN A row of houses in the middle of the street.	4G		BH
MIDDLESEX STREET see: Hog Lane, Portsoken			
MIDDLE TEMPLE An Inn of Court for the study and practice of the law. See also under Temple.	5G		BH
MIDDLE TEMPLE LANE	5G		BH
MILFORD LANE Mylforth la; —; —	5F		BH
MILK STREET Mylke streat; —; —	4M	CE2	BH
MILL LANE Name shown on Morgan's map.	8U		BH
MILTON STREET see: Grub Street			
MINCING LANE Mynchen lane; Mynchin lane; —	5S	CE2	BH
MINORIES The Minoris; —; Mynores	4U,5U		BH
MOLESTRAND DOCK	7L		BH
MONKWELL STREET Muggle st; —; —	3M		BH
MONTE JOVIS INN	5T		BH
MOORFIELDS More Fyeld; MOOR FIELD; —	3P,3Q	CE1	BH
MOORGATE (GATE) (G4) More Gate; MOOR GATE; Moor Gate	3P	CE1	BH
MOORGATE (STREET) see: Little Moorfields			
MORGAN'S LANE	8V		BH
MOUNT CALVARY Named as such by Stow. On top is a windmill (X20).	1L		BH

NARROW WALL, LAMBETH — This was an embankment with a path along the top. 7C,6D,6E BH

NEEDLER'S LANE — see: Pancras Lane

NEW FISH STREET — New fyshe streate; New fische strete; — 6R CE2 BH
Also called 'Bridge Street', 'Fish Street Hill' and 'New Fish Street Hill'. The term 'New' was used to distinguish it from Old Fish Street (q.v.) in the western part of the City.

NEWGATE (GATE) (G9) — New gat; —; — 4K BH

NEWGATE MARKET — Newgat merket; —; — The market was in the middle of Newgate Street. Railings (X64) are shown. 4K BH

NEWGATE STREET — 4K,4L BH

NEW INN — An Inn of Chancery appertaining to the Middle Temple. Shown more clearly and named on Norden's map. 4F BH

NEW PALACE YARD FOUNTAIN (W20) — Marked 'fountain' on Vertue's copy of 'Agas'. 7A BH

NEW RENTS, SOUTHWARK — Now known as Cathedral Street. 8Q BH

NICHOLAS LANE — see: St. Nicholas Lane

NOBLE STREET — Noble str; —; — 3L,3M,4L BH

NORTHUMBERLAND HOUSE, ALDERSGATE — 4L BH

NORTHUMBERLAND HOUSE, ALDGATE — Stow says that the house had been vacated by the Earls of Northumberland and the gardens made into bowling alleys, dicing houses, etc. 5T BH

NORTON FOLGATE — This was a small Liberty north of and adjoining the City ward of Bishopsgate. The road leading north was (and still is) called Norton Folgate where it passed through the Liberty. 2R CE1 BH

OAT LANE — Ote la; —; — 4M BH

OLD BAILEY — Olde baily; —; — 4K,5K BH

OLD BROAD STREET — see: Broad Street

OLD CHANGE — Olde change; —; — 4L,5L BH

OLD FISH STREET — At the time of the map this name referred to the section of street from Old Change to Bow Lane. The eastern half, from Friday Street to Bow Lane, is now known as 'Great Trinity Lane'. The western part of Old Fish Street became known as 'Knightrider Street' and is so called now. 5L,5M BH

OLD FISH STREET HILL — 5M,6M BH

OLD JEWRY — Olde Iuree; Holde Jurye; — 4P CE2 BH

OLD STREET — Olde str; —; — 2L,2M BH

OLD SWAN INN — The olde Swanne; The holde swane; The holde swane 6Q CE2 BH

OLD SWAN LANE — Called 'Ebgate Lane' by Stow. 6Q CE2 BH

OLD SWAN STAIRS — 6Q CE2 BH

OLD TEMPLE (approx. site) — The original London house of the Knights Templars, before they moved to the Temple in Fleet Street (q.v.). Much of the Old Temple was pulled down in 1595. 4G BH

[OXFORD STREET] — The Waye to Vxbridge; —; — Vertue entered 'Oxford road' on his copy of 'Agas'. 3A,3B BH

PAGET HOUSE — Paget Place; —; Paget P In 1563 William Paget died and Paget House passed to the Earl of Leicester. It was then called Leicester House, the name shown on Norden's map of 1593. 5G BH

PAINTER STAINERS' HALL (approx. site) — 6M BH

PANCRAS LANE — see: St. Pancras Lane

PARDON CHURCHYARD — Used for the burial of victims of the Black Death 1348-9. 2K BH

PARIS GARDEN — Paris Garden; —; Parys Gardeÿn This was an old manor 7J BH

PARIS GARDEN MANOR HOUSE — 7H BH

PARIS GARDEN STAIRS — 7J BH

PATERNOSTER ROW — Patern̄r Row; —; — 5K,5L BH

PAULET HOUSE — see: Winchester House, Broad Street 4L BH

Entry	Ref		
PAUL'S CHAIN — Paules chayne; —; — Strictly speaking, Paul's Chain was the section of road N. out of Carter Lane to St. Paul's Churchyard. The rest of the road was called 'Paul's Wharf Hill'. The labelling on the map would therefore appear to be in error.	5L,6L		BH
PAUL'S WHARF — Poles Wharfe; —; Powles warf	6L		BH
PAUL'S WHARF HILL — see: Paul's Chain			
PETER'S HILL — see: St. Peter's Hill			
PETTICOAT LANE — see: Hog Lane, Portsoken			
PETTY FRANCE	3R	CE1	BH
PETTY WALES — Petit Walas; —; —	6T		BH
PEWTERERS' HALL (approx. site)	5R	CE2	BH
PHILIP LANE	3M		BH
PHILPOT LANE — Fylpot lane; Fillepott lane; — Sometimes known as 'St. Andrew Hubbard Lane'.	5R	CE2	BH
[PICCADILLY] — The Waye to Redinge; —; — The name Piccadilly was not in use until about 1624.	3A		BH
PICKERING HOUSE — A 'faire greate house, builded by Sir William Pickering' (Stow).	4R	CE2	BH
PIE CORNER — Pie corner	4K		BH
PIKE GARDEN, SOUTHWARK — Four fish ponds are shown.	8L		BH

Entry	Ref		
PINNERS' HALL — see: Plasterers' Hall			
PISSING ALLEY — Pissing la; —; — Not mentioned by Stow. It seems that Basing Lane extended W. to include this alley. The alley was later called 'Little Friday Street' and was absorbed into Cannon Street at the western extension in 1853.	5M		BH
PLASTERERS' HALL (approx. site) — The company was incorporated in 1501 and took over the Pinners' Hall in 1556.	3M		BH
PLUMBERS' HALL (approx. site)	6N	CE2	BH
POOR JEWRY — Now called Jewry Street.	4T		BH
POSTERN GATE (G1) — Postern gate; —; Postern Gate	6U		BH
POSTERN LANE, CRIPPLEGATE — see: Fore Street			
POULTNEY LANE — see: St. Laurence's Lane, Thames Street			
POULTRY	4P,5P	CE2	BH
POULTRY COMPTER (approx. site) — One of the Sheriff's Prisons.	4P	CE2	BH
PRIVY STAIRS — Preuy bridge; —; Prenÿ bredge These stairs were part of Whitehall Palace.	6B		BH
PUDDING LANE — Puddinge la; Puding l; — Stow calls it 'Rother Lane'.	6R	CE2	BH
PUDDING MILL (X116) — A water mill.	7J		BH
PUDDING MILL STREAM (X215)	8J		BH

Entry	Ref		
PUDDLE DOCK HILL — see: St. Andrew's Hill			
PUDDLE WHARF — Later known as Puddle Dock.	6K		BH
QUEENHITHE — Queenehyue; HYVE; Quenehyue Only half the dock (and therefore half the name) is to be seen on CE2.	6M	CE2	BH
QUEEN'S BRIDGE — The Queenes bridge; —; Ys Queenes Bredge Later called 'Parliament Stairs'.	8A		BH
REDCROSS STREET — Redcros str; —; —	2L,2M, 3M		BH
[RED LION FIELDS]	3F		BH
ROLLS HOUSE — The place where the rolls and records of the Court of Chancery were kept.	4G,5G		BH
ROMELAND, BILLINGSGATE — A coal market.	6S	CE2	BH
ROOD LANE — Roode lane; Roude lane; —	5S,6S	CE2	BH
ROSE, MANOR OF — According to Stow 'an house, sometime belonging to the Duke of Buckingham, wherein the said school is kept' (this being the Merchant Taylors' School, founded in 1561).	6Q	CE2	BH
ROYAL EXCHANGE — Erected between 1566 and 1570. It is clearly shown on the 'Agas' map with a weather vane (X50) in the shape of a grasshopper, the emblem of Sir Thomas Gresham, its founder. The building has been inserted into the map as an after-	4Q		

Entry	Grid		
ROYAL MEWS, WESTMINSTER — Vertue wrote 'Mewes' on his copy of the 'Agas' map. These were the Royal Stables.	4B,5B		BH
ROYAL STREET see: College Hill			
SADDLERS' HALL (approx. site)	4M		BH
[SAFFRON HILL] Called 'Gold lane' by Stow.	3H,3J,4J		BH
ST. ALBAN, WOOD STREET — S. Alban; —; 'Agas' map number 19.	3M		BH
ST. ALBAN'S COURT	3M,4M		
ST. ALPHAGE — S. Tapius; S. Thaphins; S. Thaphins 'Agas' map number 21.	3M	CE1	BH
ST. ANDREW BY THE WARDROBE	6K		BH
ST. ANDREW, HOLBORN, AND CHURCHYARD — S. Andreus; —;	4H		BH
ST. ANDREW HUBBARD, AND CHURCHYARD	6R	CE2	BH
ST. ANDREW'S HILL — S. Andrewes hyll; —; — Also known as Puddle Dock Hill.	5K,6K		BH
ST. ANDREW UNDERSHAFT, AND CHURCHYARD — S. Andrewe vnder shafte; S And. vnder chaft; — 'Agas' map number 30.	4S	CE2	BH

Entry	Grid		
thought indicating that the 'Agas' map was probably prepared before the Exchange was completed. The Royal Exchange is not shown on CE2 or the first state of BH, but does appear on later states of BH.			
ST. ANNE & ST. AGNES, AND CHURCHYARD — Also known as 'St. Anne in the Willows'.	4L		BH
ST. ANNE'S LANE — S. Anne la; —; Now called Gresham Street.	4L		BH
ST. ANTHOLIN, AND CHURCHYARD — 'Agas' map letter Z, shown reversed.	5N	CE2	BH
ST. ANTHONY — S. Anthony; S. Anthony; — The hospital of St. Anthony was despoiled after the Dissolution and the church was let to French Protestants during Elizabeth's reign.	4Q	CE2	BH
ST. AUDOEN — Not shown. It stood on the E. side of Warwick Lane at the junction with Newgate Street. Demolished soon after 1547 and its parish united with two others to form the parish of Christ Church (q.v.).	(4K)		BH
ST. AUGUSTINE INN — Described as being next to the Bridge House and E. of St. Olave's church, the Inn of the abbots of St. Augustine, Canterbury, is probably represented on 'Agas' by the house with the large doorway.	8S		BH
ST. AUGUSTINE PAPEY, AND CHURCHYARD — Papye; PAPYE; — The brotherhood was suppressed in 1548 and the church removed soon after.	4R,4S	CE1	BH
ST. AUGUSTINE, WATLING STREET — 'Agas' map number 11.	5L		BH

Entry	Grid		
ST. BARTHOLOMEW BY THE EXCHANGE, AND CHURCHYARD — CE2 shows a chapel built beside the church at the S.E. corner. The chapel was added by Sir William Capel in 1509.	4Q	CE2	BH
ST. BARTHOLOMEW'S HOSPITAL	3K,4K		BH
ST. BARTHOLOMEW THE GREAT, AND CHURCHYARD — S. Bartholome; —; St. Barth Originally the church of the Augustinian monastery of St. Bartholomew, it became a parish church in 1544. Only the choir of the church is shown; the nave (which extended west to Smithfield) was demolished in 1539.	3K,3L		BH
ST. BARTHOLOMEW THE LESS — 'Agas' map number 32. A parish church for tenants dwelling within the precinct of St. Bartholomew's Hospital.	3K		BH
ST. BENET FINK — 'Agas' map number 26.	4Q	CE2	BH
ST. BENET, GRACECHURCH STREET — On 'Agas' the name 'S. Denys' is engraved immediately above St. Benet's Church, but refers to the church of St. Dionis which is situated further east.	5R	CE2	BH
ST. BENET, PAUL'S WHARF — The name 'S. Perer' drawn on the 'Agas' map below the church applies to the next church due E. which is St. Peter, Paul's Wharf.	6L		BH
ST. BENET SHEREHOG — The church is called 'St. Sithes' by Stow.	5N	CE2	BH
ST. BENNET'S HILL see: Paul's Chaine			

ST. BOTOLPH, ALDERSGATE, AND CHURCHYARD

—; —; S. Bwttols

'Agas' map number 31. — 3L — BH

ST. BOTOLPH, ALDGATE, AND CHURCHYARD

S. Buttolphes; —; S. Bwttols — 4U — BH

ST. BOTOLPH, BILLINGSGATE

'Agas' map letter E, shown reversed. — 6R — CE2 — BH

ST. BOTOLPH, BISHOPSGATE, AND CHURCHYARD

S. Buttolphes; S. Bwttols

Both CE1 and BH show a cross in the churchyard. It is known from Machyn's Diary that this cross was destroyed in August 1559. — 3R — CE1 — BH

ST. BRIDE, AND CHURCHYARD

'Agas' map letter C. — 5J — BH

ST. CHRISTOPHER LE STOCKS — 4P — CE2 — BH

ST. CLARE, ABBEY OF (approx. site)

Surrendered 1538 and the site granted to the Bishops of Bath for their town house. By Stow's time, large storehouses for armour had been built here. — 4U — BH

ST. CLEMENT DANES, AND CHURCHYARD

S. Clement; —; — — 5F — BH

ST. CLEMENT, EASTCHEAP

'Agas' map letter F, drawn on its side. — 5Q — CE2 — BH

ST. CLEMENT'S LANE

S. Clement lane; S. Clement l; —

Now called Clement's Lane. — 5Q — CE2 — BH

ST. DIONIS BACKCHURCH, AND CHURCHYARD

S. Denys; S. Denys; S. Denys — 5R — CE2 — BH

ST. DUNSTAN IN THE EAST, AND CHURCHYARD — 6S — CE2 — BH

ST. DUNSTAN IN THE WEST, AND CHURCHYARD

S. Dōstō in the West; —; — — 5G — BH

ST. DUNSTAN'S HILL

S. Donat hyll; S. Donestn hyll; —

The part of the road to the W. of the church was also called 'Church Lane'. This part is now known as Idol Lane. — 6S — CE2 — BH

ST. DUNSTAN'S LANE

see: Fowle Lane

ST. EDMUND, LOMBARD STREET — 5Q — CE2 — BH

ST. EDMUND THE BISHOP AND MARY MAGDALEN, CHARNEL HOUSE AND CHAPEL OF (X171) — 2R — CE1 — BH

ST. ETHELBURGA — 4R — CE1&2 — BH

ST. EWIN

see: St. Audoen

ST. GABRIEL FENCHURCH, AND CHURCHYARD

Fen church; Fans Churen; Fäs Churi

The church stood in the middle of the road. The churchyard is indicated by a cross (X46). — 5S — CE2 — BH

ST. GEORGE, BOTOLPH LANE — 6R — CE2 — BH

ST. GEORGE'S LANE

S. Georg la.; —; — — 6R — CE2 — BH

ST. GILES, CRIPPLEGATE, AND CHURCHYARD

S. Giles; —; S. Gilles — 3M — BH

[ST. GILES HIGH STREET]

The streets and lanes around St. Giles, as shown on 'Agas' and BH, bear little resemblance to those shown on a large scale manuscript plan of the area made in 1585. — 3C — BH

ST. GILES IN THE FIELDS

S. Gyles in the Fyeld; —; S. Gyles — 3C — BH

---

ni the Fÿeldes

Formerly a hospital chapel, it became a parochial church after the Dissolution.

ST. GREGORY-BY-ST. PAUL'S, AND CHURCHYARD — 5L — BH

ST. HELEN, AND CHURCHYARD

S. Elen; S. helenes; —

This became a parish church at the Dissolution of the Monasteries. Before then it had been the church of the Priory of St. Helen. Immediately W. of the name 'S. Elen' is shown the old gatehouse to the priory church with a cross on top. There is a cross (X44) in the churchyard. — 4R — CE2 — BH

ST. HELEN'S WELL (W16) — 4R — CE2 — BH

ST. JAMES, CLERKENWELL — 2J — BH

ST. JAMES GARLICKHITHE

'Agas' map number 1. — 6N — CE2 — BH

ST. JAMES IN THE WALL HERMITAGE — 3M — BH

ST. JAMES'S PARK

S. Jemes Parke; —; —

The area with a fence around it is named on Vertue's map as 'Spring Garden' (X107) and the houses (X106) are named on Norden's plan as 'the Park Lodgings'. — 5A — BH

ST. JOHN, PRIORY OF

—; —; S. Iohns

In 1549 most of the church was blown up by gunpowder and the stones used to build old Somerset House. Parts of the building were repaired in Mary's reign. — 2J — BH

ST. JOHN'S LANE

S. John st; —; — — 3J — BH

ST. JOHN STREET — 1J,2J — BH

Entry and notes	Map ref.	Sources
ST. JOHN THE BAPTIST, WALBROOK — S. Iohne in Walbroke; S. Iohons in W; — 'Agas' map letter W.	6P	CE2 BH
ST. JOHN THE EVANGELIST — 'Agas' map number 10.	5M	BH
ST. JOHN ZACHARY — 'Agas' map number 17.	4M	BH
ST. KATHERINE COLEMAN — S. Katerio colmans; —; Kat Colmās	5T	BH
ST. KATHERINE CREE, AND CHURCHYARD — Churchyard indicated by a cross (X45).	4S	CE2 BH
ST. KATHERINE'S HERMITAGE (approx. site)	5B	BH
ST. KATHERINE'S HOSPITAL — S. Kateren; —; S. Katheř. The hospital was suppressed by Henry VIII but reconstituted by Queen Elizabeth. The gateway (X93) is shown. Part of the church is shown to the right of the name but it does not appear on the Guildhall copy of the 'Agas' map.	6W	BH
ST. KATHERINE'S LANE — S. Katerens la.; —; —	6W	BH
ST. KATHERINE'S STAIRS	6W	BH
ST. LAURENCE HILL, THAMES STREET — S. Laurens hyll; S. Lorens hyll; — Called 'Poultney lane' by Stow, it is now called 'Laurence Pountney Lane'.	6Q	CE2 BH
ST. LAURENCE LANE, GUILDHALL — S. Laurence lane; St. Lorens lane; — Now called 'Lawrence Lane'.	4N	CE2 BH
ST. LAURENCE LANE, THAMES STREET — It is now called Ducksfoot Lane.	6Q	BH
ST. LAURENCE POUNTNEY HILL — S. Laurence ponie; —; Called 'St. Laurence Hill' by Stow. Now called 'Laurence Pountney Hill'.	6Q	BH
ST. LAWRENCE, JEWRY — —; S. Laureñs; — 'Agas' map number 23.	4N	CE2 BH
ST. LAWRENCE POULTNEY, AND CHURCHYARD — 'Agas' map letter N.	6Q	CE2 BH
ST. LEONARD, EASTCHEAP — Not shown. It stood on S. side of Little Eastcheap at junction with New Fish Street.	(6R)	BH
ST. LEONARD, FOSTER LANE — The church stood on the W. side of Foster Lane almost opposite St. Vedast. The map shows a tower (X195) which could represent this church. The tower is, however, placed too far W. and more probably represents the church of St. Martins-le-Grand (q.v.).	(4L)	BH
ST. LEONARD, SHOREDITCH	1R	BH
ST. MAGNUS THE MARTYR, AND CHURCHYARD — S. mangnus; S. Magnus; —	6R	CE2 BH
ST. MARGARET, LOTHBURY — S. Marget; S. Margette; —	4P	CE2 BH
ST. MARGARET MOSES — 'Agas' map number 9.	5M	BH
ST. MARGARET, NEW FISH STREET, AND CHURCHYARD	6R	CE2 BH
ST. MARGARET PATTENS, AND CHURCHYARD — S. Margarits patens; —; —	6S	CE2 BH
'Agas' map letter D, shown reversed. The name, only given on the 'Agas' map, is some distance W. of the church.		
ST. MARGARET, WESTMINSTER, AND CHURCHYARD	7A	BH
ST. MARTIN-IN-THE-FIELDS, AND CHURCHYARD — S. Martin's; —; — The 'Agas' label 'S. Martin's' may represent the church or the street. Vertue has entered 'S. Martins lane' here on his copy of the 'Agas' map.	4C	BH
ST. MARTIN, LUDGATE — 'Agas' map number 14.	5K	BH
ST. MARTIN ORGAR — The tower (X196) is almost certainly meant to represent the church of St. Martin Orgar. It should be drawn further W., on the E. side of St. Martin's Lane. The same error occurs on CE2.	6R	CE2 BH
ST. MARTIN OUTWICH	4R	CE2 BH
ST. MARTIN POMARY	4N	CE2 BH
ST. MARTIN'S FIELD — The name of 'St. Martins field' is given on a manuscript map of 1585.	3B,4B	BH
ST. MARTIN'S LANE, STRAND	3B,4B, 4C,5C	BH
ST. MARTIN'S LANE, THAMES STREET — S. Martines la; Martins l; — Now called Martin Lane.	6Q	CE2 BH
ST. MARTIN'S-LE-GRAND (CHURCH) — The name 'S. Martins' could refer to the street or the collegiate church of the same name. There is	(4L)	

ST. MARTIN'S-LE-GRAND (STREET)
a tower (X195) shown which could represent the church and to the N. is a courtyard (X78) which could also be part of the old precinct. The church was taken down c.1548.

ST. MARTIN'S-LE-GRAND (STREET)
S. Martins; —; —
Called 'St. Martin's lane' by Stow. — 4L — BH

ST. MARTIN, VINTRY
S. Martin; S. Martins; —
'Agas' map letter Y. — 6N — CE2 — BH

ST. MARY ABCHURCH
'Agas' map letter U. — 5Q — CE2 — BH

ST. MARY, ALDERMANBURY, AND CHURCHYARD
'Agas' map number 20, the '2' is reversed. — 3M — CE1 — BH

ST. MARY ALDERMARY
'Agas' map number 3, shown reversed. This church is obviously drawn conventionally. Stow says the church was rebuilt in the early 16th century, and that the tower was still only 15 to 20 feet high when he was writing. — 5N — CE2 — BH

ST. MARY-AT-HILL (CHURCH)
Not shown. Situated on E. side of Love Lane. — (6S)

ST. MARY-AT-HILL (STREET)
S. Mary hyll; S. Mary hyll; — — 6S — CE2 — BH

ST. MARY AXE (CHURCH), AND CHURCHYARD
In c.1565 the parish was united with St. Andrew Undershaft, the church having fallen into disrepair. The building became a warehouse. — 4R — CE2 — BH

ST. MARY AXE (STREET)
S. Marie axe; S. Ma. Axe; — — 4R — CE2 — BH

ST. MARY BOTHAW
'Agas' map letter T. — 6P — CE2 — BH

ST. MARY BOTOLPH LANE
S. Mariebutolph la; —; —
Later called Turnwheel Lane. — 6P — CE2 — BH

ST. MARY CLERKENWELL, NUNNERY OF
Suppressed by Henry VIII in 1539. The buildings survived intact for a number of years. — 2H — BH

ST. MARY COLECHURCH
Not shown. It stood at the S. end of Old Jewry on the W. corner. — (4N)

ST. MARY GRACES, ABBEY OF (approx. site)
This Cistercian abbey, sometimes called Eastminster, was suppressed in 1539 and the site granted to Sir Arthur D'arcy who demolished the buildings of the abbey and erected a storehouse for victuals. — 5W — BH

ST. MARY, ISLINGTON — 1K

ST. MARY, LAMBETH
See notes on Lambeth. — 8C — BH

ST. MARY-LE-BOW, AND CHURCHYARD
Bowe church; Bow Chur'; —
'Agas' map number 4, shown reversed. — 4M,5M — CE2 — BH

ST. MARY-LE-STRAND
Not shown. Pulled down in 1544 to make room for Somerset House.

ST. MARY MAGDALEN, GUILDHALL, CHAPEL OF
see: Guildhall Chapel

ST. MARY MAGDALEN, MILK STREET
'Agas' map number 16, the '6' is reversed. — 4M — CE2 — BH

ST. MARY MAGDALEN, OLD FISH STREET
'Agas' map number 13. — 5L — BH

ST. MARY MOUNTHAW
Not shown. It stood on the W. side of Old Fish Street Hill towards the S. end. — (6M)

ST. MARY OVERIE'S DOCK — 8Q — BH

ST. MARY OVERIE, SOUTHWARK
see: St. Saviour, Southwark

ST. MARY OVERY STAIRS
Known later as 'St. Saviour's Stairs'. — 7Q — BH

ST. MARY ROUNCEVAL (approx. site)
Surrendered in 1544, this Augustinian hospital for the poor came into the possession of John Rede who converted the chapel and great chamber into a residence and built several new tenements. — 5B — BH

ST. MARY SOMERSET, AND CHURCHYARD
S. Mary Somerset; —; —
'Agas' map number 7. — 6M — BH

ST. MARY SPITAL, PRIORY OF
—; S. Ma. Spittel; —
Surrendered to Henry VIII but the churchyard and some buildings remained for many years, including the pulpit cross (X82). — 2R — CE1 — BH

ST. MARY STAINING
'Agas' map number 18. — 3M — BH

ST. MARY WOOLCHURCH, AND CHURCHYARD
Wollchur; —; —
'Agas' map letter Q. The church was also known as 'St. Mary Woolchurch Haw' and 'St. Mary at Stocks'. — 5P — CE2 — BH

ST. MARY WOOLNOTH
'Agas' map letter P, shown reversed. — 5Q — CE2 — BH

ST. MATTHEW, FRIDAY STREET
The closely-spaced horizontal lines drawn on this tower are not found — 4M — BH

Entry	Ref	CE	BH
on any other tower on the 'Agas' map, and could indicate that it was made of wood.			
ST. MICHAEL BASSISHAW —; S. Mignells; — 'Agas' map number 22.	3N	CE1	BH
ST. MICHAEL, CORNHILL 'Agas' map number 27.	4Q	CE2	BH
ST. MICHAEL, CROOKED LANE, AND CHURCHYARD —; S. Miguells; — 'Agas' map letter K, shown reversed.	6Q,6R	CE2	BH
ST. MICHAEL LE QUERNE	4L		BH
ST. MICHAEL PATERNOSTER ROYAL 'Agas' map number 3, shown reversed.	6N	CE2	BH
ST. MICHAEL, QUEENHITHE 'Agas' map number 6.	6M		BH
ST. MICHAEL'S LANE	6Q		BH
ST. MICHAEL, WOOD STREET	4M		BH
ST. MILDRED, BREAD STREET Not shown. It stood on the E. side of Bread Street and on the N. side of the junction with Basing Lane.	(5M)		
ST. MILDRED, POULTRY 'Agas' map number 25. Note the weather vane in the form of a sailing ship on CE2.	4P	CE2	BH
ST. NICHOLAS ACON Not shown. It stood on the W. side of St. Nicholas Lane towards the northern end.	(5Q)		
ST. NICHOLAS COLE ABBEY 'Agas' map number 12.	5M		BH
ST. NICHOLAS LANE S. Nycolas lane; S. Niccolas l; — Now called Nicholas Lane.	5Q	CE2	BH
ST. NICHOLAS OLAVE 'Agas' map number 8.	5M		BH
ST. NICHOLAS SHAMBLES S. N. Shambles; —; — Not shown. Church taken down and houses built on the site c.1547.	(4L)		BH
ST. OLAVE, HART STREET 'Agas' map letter A.	5T	CE2	BH
ST. OLAVE, OLD JEWRY Situated on W. side of Old Jewry.	(4P)	CE2	
ST. OLAVE, SILVER STREET Not shown. It stood on S. side of Silver Street at the western end.	(3M)		
ST. OLAVE, TOOLEY STREET S. Towlles; —; St. Towlles	7S		BH
ST. PANCRAS LANE S. Pancraes la.; —; — Stow calls this 'Needlers lane'. It is now called Pancras Lane.	5N	CE2	
ST. PANCRAS, SOPER LANE 'Agas' map letter X. This tower probably represents the church of St. Pancras, Soper Lane. If so it should have been drawn on the N. side of St. Pancras Lane a little W. of the church of St. Benet Sherehog.	5N	CE2	
ST. PAUL'S CATHEDRAL Poles church; —; S. Paule The spire, which was destroyed by lightning in 1561, is shown on BH but not on 'Agas'.	4L,5L		BH
ST. PAUL'S CHURCHYARD	5L		BH
ST. PAUL'S CROSS (X83) Originally the site of a stone cross, a stone pulpit was built here in the fifteenth century.	5L		BH
ST. PAUL'S SCHOOL (approx. site) It stood on the W. side of Old Change.	5L		
ST. PETER AD VINCULA	6U		BH
ST. PETER, CORNHILL S. Peter; St. P; — 'Agas' map number 29.	4R	CE2	BH
ST. PETER LE POOR 'Agas' map number 24.	4Q	CE2	
ST. PETER, PAUL'S WHARF S. Perer; —; — On 'Agas' the name is drawn below the church of St. Benet, Paul's Wharf.	6L		BH
ST. PETER'S HILL S. Peter hyll; —; — Now called Peter's Hill.	5L,6L		BH
ST. PETER, WESTCHEAP 'Agas' map number 15.	4M		BH
ST. SAVIOUR, SOUTHWARK, AND CHURCHYARD S. Mary owber; —; S. Marÿ ouerÿs This church had been part of the Priory of St. Mary Overy. In 1540 the priory was surrendered to Henry VIII.	8Q,8R		BH
ST. SEPULCHRE, AND CHURCHYARD 'Agas' map number 34. Only part of the church tower can be seen on the Guildhall copy of the 'Agas' map. The Pepysian Library copy shows further details of the church where the number 34 is clearly visible on the tower.	4J,4K		BH
ST. SEPULCHRE'S ALLEY	4K		BH
ST. SITHES see: St. Benet Sherehog			
ST. STEPHEN, COLEMAN STREET Not shown. It should be on the W. side of Coleman Street towards the S. end.	(4P)		

ST. STEPHEN, WALBROOK 'Agas' map letter R.	5P	CE2	BH
ST. SWITHIN, LONDON STONE 'Agas' map letter S.	5P	CE2	BH
ST. SWITHIN'S LANE S. Swytins lane; S. Southins l; —	5Q	CE2	BH
ST. SYTHES see: St. Benet Sherehog			
ST. SYTHE'S LANE S. Syches lane; S. Siffets lane; — Now called Sise Lane.	5N	CE2	BH
ST. THOMAS APOSTLE (CHURCH) S. Thomas Apostel; S Thomas apostell; — 'Agas' map letter Z, shown reversed.	5N	CE2	BH
ST. THOMAS OF ACON see: Mercers' Hall			
ST. THOMAS'S HOSPITAL After the Dissolution the former almonry was purchased by the citizens of London who repaired and enlarged it. It was opened for the reception of the sick poor in 1552. The building marked in red as 'St. Thomas Hospital' may be Lewes Inn, which Stow describes as having 'arched gates'.	8S		BH
ST. VEDAST	4M		BH
SALISBURY COURT Salisburie Co.; —; —	5J		
SALISBURY HOUSE Also known as Salisbury Inn the land and buildings were originally the property of the Bishop of Salisbury. Bought by Sir Richard Sackville in 1564.	5J,6J		BH
SALTERS' HALL (approx. site)	5M		BH
SALT WHARF, QUEENHITHE	6M		BH
SARACEN'S HEAD 'A fayre and large Inne for receipt of travellers' (Stow).	4J		
SAVOY PALACE Sauoye; —; Sauoye Used as a hospital for the poor at the time of the map.	5D		BH
SAVOY PALACE, GREAT GATE OF 'Agas' map letter B.	5D		
SCAVENGER'S CLOSE This name appears on a map of 1585.	3A,4A		BH
SCOTLAND YARD 'A large plotte of ground inclosed with bricke . . . where great buildings hath beene for receipt of the Kings of Scotland and other estates of that countrey . . .' (Stow).	5B,5C		BH
SCROPE'S INN, HOLBORN Formerly an inn of Serjeants-at-Law, it was demised to John Scrope and others in the reign of Henry VIII.	4H,4J		BH
SEACOAL LANE Seacole la; —; —	4J		BH
SEETHING LANE Sethinge la; —; — Stow calls it 'Sydon Lane' or 'Sidon Lane'.	5T,6T	CE2	BH
SERJEANT'S INN An Inn of Serjeants-at-Law.	5H		BH
SERMON LANE Sermon la; —; —	5L		
[SHAFTESBURY AVENUE] The stretch of road south of St. Giles Church between St. Martin's Lane and St. Giles High Street follows the course of what is now Shaftesbury Avenue. Comparison with the 1585 manuscript plan shows that the continuation of this lane westwards is inaccurately drawn on 'Agas' and BH.	3C		BH
SHAMBLES, THE S. N. Shambles; —; — Stow calls this street 'Mount Godard Street'.	4L		BH
SHERBORNE LANE Schyrbur la; Sheborg l; —	5Q	CE2	BH
SHIRE LANE	5G		BH
SHOE LANE Schow lane; —; —	4J,5J		BH
SHOREDITCH	1R,2R		
SHOREDITCH (STREET) Shordiche; SHORDICHE; — The road leading from Bishopsgate was called Norton Folgate for a short section and then simply 'Shoreditch'.	1R,2R	CE1	
SHREWSBURY HOUSE see: Coldharbour			
SILVER STREET Syluer str; —; —	3M		BH
SISE LANE see: St. Sythe's Lane			
SKINNERS' HALL Surmised from the garden shown.	6P	CE2	BH
SLAUGHTER HOUSE —; —; The Slaughter howse (opposite Lambeth Palace)			BH
SMART'S KEY Smarc kay; —; —	7S		BH
SMITHFIELD Schmyt Fyeld; —; Smÿthe Fyeld An open area of nearly 6 acres, used as a market for sheep, horses, cattle and hay.	3K		BH

SMITHFIELD BARS (X62) A wooden barrier marking the boundary of the City.	3K		
SMITHFIELD STREET see: Cow Lane			
SNOW HILL Called 'Snor hill' by Stow.	4J,4K		BH
SOMAR'S KEY Somers kay; —; Somers k	7S		BH
SOMERSET HOUSE Somerset Place; —; Somerset Place Palace built by the Duke of Somerset, Lord Protector. Construction commenced in 1546-7. The inns of the Bishops of Chester Llandaff, Lichfield, Coventry and Worcester, including the old church of St. Mary le Strand, were demolished to make space.	5E		BH
SOPER'S LANE Soper lane; Sopper lane; — It is now the northern part of Queen Street.	5N	CE2	BH
SOUTHAMPTON HOUSE Originally the manor house of the Blemunds (from which the name Bloomsbury is derived), it later came into the possession of the Earl of Southampton. It stood on the site of what is now Bloomsbury Square.	3E		BH
SOUTHAMPTON HOUSE (approx. site) Formerly the Bishop of Lincoln's London residence, it came into the hands of the Earls of Southampton in Stow's time.	4G		BH
SOUTHWARK Southwake; —; South warke	8R		BH
SOUTHWARK CATHEDRAL see: St. Saviour, Southwark			
SOUTHWARK WELL	(8R)		BH
SPITALFIELDS The spitel Fyeld; THE SPITEL; The Spitel fields The wording on CE1 doubtless continues on the missing sheet due E.	2T	CE1	BH
STAINING LANE Stayning la; —; —	4M		
STANDARD, CHEAPSIDE (W2) A water conduit; also a common place of punishment for serious offences.	4M		BH
STANGATE STAIRS, LAMBETH	7C		BH
STAPLE INN An Inn of Chancery appertaining to Grays Inn.	4G		BH
STAR CHAMBER Starre Chamber; —; Stehar Chamber A judicial court in the Palace of Westminster.	7B		BH
STATIONERS' HALL (approx. site) The Company moved in 1553 from Milk Street to St. Peter's College near St. Paul's Deanery.	5K		BH
STEELYARD, THE Styllyarde; STILIARDS; Stiliards The headquarters of the Hanseatic merchants in London.	6P	CE2	BH
STOCKS MARKET Stokes; Stokes; — A market for meal and fish situated on the N. side of St. Mary Woolchurch Haw.	5P	CE2	BH
STOCKS MARKET CONDUIT (W13)	4P	CE2	BH
STRAND	4C-4E, 5C-5G		BH
STRAND LANE Strand la; —; — At the N. end, Vertue's map shows 'Strand Bridge'.	5F		BH
SUFFOLK LANE The map is rather seriously distorted in the area around the Manor of the Rose. Suffolk Lane should be a continuation of Wolsies Lane.	6Q	CE2	BH
SUFFOLK PLACE see: York House			
SWAN LANE see: Old Swan Lane			
TALLOW CHANDLERS' HALL (approx. site)	6P		
TASSELL CLOSE	2R	CE1	BH
TEMPLE, THE The Temple; —; The Temple A liberty or district between Fleet Street and the Thames, so called from the Knights Templars who settled here in 1184. The Inner and Middle Temples were leased to students of the Common Law from the early 14th century onwards.	5G		BH
TEMPLE BAR Temple barre; —; — A wooden gateway marking the western limit of the City.	5G		BH
TEMPLE CHURCH Temple; —; —	5G		BH
TEMPLE GARDENS	5G		BH
[TEMPLE LANE]	5H		BH
TEMPLE STAIRS	6G		BH

THAMES STREET 6K-6T CE2 BH
Tames streate, Tames str; Tamys strete; —
Now called Upper Thames Street to the W. of London Bridge and Lower Thames Street to the E.

THAVIES INN 4H BH
Purchased by the Society of Lincoln's Inn, 1550, for the use of law students.

[THEOBALDS ROAD] 3G BH

THREADNEEDLE STREET 4P-4R CE2 BH

THREADNEEDLE STREET WELL (W12) 4Q CE2 BH
It was a pump by Stow's time.

THREE CRANES LANE 6N CE2 BH

THREE CRANES STAIRS 6N CE2 BH

THREE CRANES WHARF 6N CE2 BH
Thre Crañs; Thre Crane; Thre Crane
This was the river frontage of the Vintry, where French wine was unloaded. The three cranes can be seen: X17, X18 and X19.

[THROGMORTON STREET] 4Q CE2 BH
Formed part of Broad Street in the mid-16th century.

TIMBERHITHE 6M BH

TOOLEY STREET 8S-8V BH
Barms strete; —; —
The street names on 'Agas' are confused here. See Bermondsey Street.

[TOTTENHAM COURT ROAD] 2B,3B BH
This lane led to the manor of Tottenham Court.

TOWER HILL 5T,6T BH
Towre hyll; —; Towre Hyl
Also known as Great Tower Hill. See also Little Tower Hill.

TOWER OF LONDON 6U,6V BH
The Towre of London; —; THE TOWRE
The representation of the Tower of London on the east side seems rather inaccurate.

TOWER ROYAL 5N BH
Toure rouial; —; —

TOWER STREET 6S,6T CE2 BH
Towre streate; Towre strete; —
Later known as Great Tower Street.

TOWNSEND LANE 2H BH

TRIG LANE 6L BH
Trygdane; —; —

TRINITY LANE 6M CE2 BH
Trinitie lane; Trinitie lane; —
Now called 'Little Trinity Lane'

TURNAGAIN LANE 4J BH
Turne agen la; —; —

TURNBASE LANE 5N CE2 BH
Turnebas la; Tornbasse l; —

TURNMILL BROOK
see: Fleet River
Stow refers to the River Fleet N. of Holborn Bridge as 'Turnmill Brook'.

TURNMILL STREET 2J,3J BH
Turner str; —; —

TURNWHEEL LANE BH
see: St. Mary Botolph Lane

TYLERS' HALL (approx. site) 3Q CE1 BH

UPPER GROUND 7H BH

UPPER THAMES STREET
see: Thames Street

VINTNERS' HALL (approx. site) 6N CE2 BH

VINTRY 6N CE2 BH
An area between St. Martin Vintry Church and the river where wine was unloaded and stored.

WALBROOK (RIVER)
Once a stream of some size and importance, it had been virtually completely filled in and vaulted over by the time the 'Agas' map was compiled, and it is certainly not visible on 'Agas', CE or BH. It flowed N.-S. from Moorfields, roughly along the line of Walbrook and Dowgate.

WALBROOK (STREET) 5P CE2 BH
Wallbrooke; Wall Brouke; —

WARWICK LANE 4K,5K BH
Wurwik la; —; —

WATERGATE 6T BH

WATER LANE, BLACKFRIARS 6K BH

WATER LANE, FLEET STREET 5H,6H BH
Water la; —; —
Now called Whitefriars St. & Carmelite St.

WATER LANE, THAMES STREET 6T CE2 BH
Water lane; Watter lane; —

WATERMEN'S HALL 6Q CE2 BH
The watermen used part of Coldharbour (q.v.) as their hall.

WATLING STREET 5L,5M,5N CE2 BH
Watlinge streat; —; —

WAX CHANDLERS' HALL (approx. site) 4M BH

WEAVERS' HALL 3N BH
Surmised from garden shown.

[WENTWORTH LANE] 3S,3T BH
Called Wentworth Street today.

WESTCHEAP
see: Cheapside

WESTMINSTER — 7A — BH
Westmynster; —; West Muster

WESTMINSTER ABBEY — 8A — BH
Known more correctly as 'the Collegiate Church of St. Peter, Westminster'. The dissolution of the monastery was effected in 1540.

WESTMINSTER HALL — 7A — BH
Westmynster hall; —; —
The old hall of the Palace of Westminster, where Law Courts were held. Six flying buttresses can be seen on the W. side.

WESTMINSTER PALACE — 7A,8A — BH
The olde Palaice; —; —
The principal seat and palace of the Kings of England from Edward the Confessor until 1512 when the bulk of the building was destroyed by fire.

WESTMINSTER SCHOOL — 8A — BH

WESTMINSTER STAIRS — 7B — BH
Named as such on Morgan's map. Called 'Kings bridge' on the map of Westminster by Norden.

[WHITCOMB STREET] — 4A — BH

WHITECHAPEL — 4W — BH
—; Whyt
Known now as Whitechapel High Street.

WHITECROSS STREET — 2M,3M — BH
Whitcros str; —; —

WHITEFRIARS — 6H — BH
Whyte Fryers; —; Whyt freres
A precinct extending from Fleet Street to the Thames comprising the site of the former House of Carmelite, or White, Friars. This had been dissolved by Henry VIII who granted the buildings to Dr. William Butte.

[WHITEHALL] — 5B,6B — BH
Then known as King St.

WHITEHALL PALACE — 6B — BH
The Courte; —; The Corte
The Palace of the Kings of England from Henry VIII to William III.

WHITEHALL STAIRS — 6B — BH
Called 'Whitehall bridge' on Norden's map.

WHITTINGTON COLLEGE (approx. site) — 6N
Whytyngton Colleage; Winthn. College; —
See also College Hill. The college stood on the N.E. side of St. Michael's Church. It was suppressed by Edward VI but the almshouses remained.

WHYTYNGTON COLLEAGE — 8A — BH
see: Whittington College

WINCHESTER HOUSE, BROAD STREET — 3Q — CE1 — BH
Land obtained in 1548 by William Paulet, Marquis of Winchester. It had been part of the Austin Friars' land (q.v.).

WINCHESTER HOUSE, SOUTHWARK — 8Q — BH
Whin chster plr; —; Wyuchester Ps
The London residence of the Bishop of Winchester. The bishop's land, which extended westwards to Paris Garden, was known as the 'Liberty of the Clink'.

WINDGOOSE LANE — 6Q — CE2

WINDMILL TAVERN (approx. site) — 4P — CE2
—; Wyndmyll; —

WINDSOR HOUSE — 3M — BH
A large mansion belonging to Lord Windsor. Also known as Nevill's Inn, after the previous owner.

WOLSIES LANE — 6Q — BH

WOODROFFE LANE — 5T — BH
Woodross la; —; —
Now known as Coopers Row.

WOOD STREET — 3M,4M — BH
Wood streat; —; —
The section from Addle Street to Cheapside was also known as 'Great Wood Street'. The section N. from Addle Street was called 'Little Wood Street'.

WOOD STREET COMPTER (approx. site) — 4M — BH
One of the Sheriff's Prisons. Moved to this site from Bread Street in 1555.

WOOL KEY — 7T — BH
—; —; Woll k

WORCESTER HOUSE — 6N — CE2 — BH
Once the residence of the Earl of Worcester, it was 'divided into many tenements' in Stow's time.

WORMWOOD STREET — 3Q,3R — BH

WORSHIP STREET
see: Hog Lane, Norton Folgate

WYCH STREET — 4F — BH

YORK HOUSE — 5C — BH
Yorke Pl; —; Suffolke P
Formerly Suffolk Place, it was acquired by the Archbishop of York in 1557 and named York House. From 1561-1603 it was leased to the Crown.

YORK STAIRS — 5C
The stairs leading to York House.

(3) GATES IN THE CITY WALL

The code numbers given to the City gates are those in R. Merrifield: *The Roman City of London* (Benn, 1965). Comments on these gates are given in the Name Index.

	Ref	CE	BH
G1—Postern Gate	6U		BH
G2—Aldgate	4T		BH
G3—Bishopsgate	3R	CE1	BH
G4—Moorgate	3P	CE1	BH
G5—Aldermanbury Postern	(3N)		
G6—Cripplegate	3M		BH
G7—West Gate of Fort	(3L)		
Blocked up by the medieval period.			
G8—Aldersgate	3L,4L		BH
G8a—Christ's Hospital Postern	4K		BH
G9—Newgate	4K		BH
G10—Ludgate	5K		BH

(4) PERSONS

	Ref	CE	BH
P1—Man and woman, out with their dog	7G		
P2—milkmaid, milking a cow	2U		
P3—archers	2U		
P4—archers	2V		
P5—laundress, laying out clothes to dry.	5V		
P6—waterbearer	6T		
He is apparently ladling water into casks carried by his two ponies.			
P7—man riding a horse.	3K		
P8—lady, child and dog.	3C		
The lady appears to be carrying something on her head.			
P9—archers	2P	CE1	
P10—archer	2N		
P11—?soldiers carrying guns.	2B		
P12—laundress laying out washing to dry	4B		
P13—laundresses laying out washing to dry	3P	CE1	
P14—laundresses laying out washing to dry	3Q		
P15—archers	2S		
P16—archers	2G		
P17—?soldier carrying gun	2S		
P18—?soldier carrying gun	2Q		
P19—?soldier carrying gun	7C		
P20—milkmaid	3U		
P21—laundress, laying out washing to dry	4A		
P22—?drovers	3K		
P23—?drovers	3K		
P24—soldiers	2S	CE1	
P25—two people taking their dog for a walk	2W		
P26—waterbearer	7P	CE2	
See also P6			

(5) WELLS, CONDUITS, PUMPS, ETC.

There are known to have been many more wells and pumps than are shown on the 'Agas' map, but only those depicted on this map have been indexed. Those appearing on the Copperplate Map but not on 'Agas' are listed at the end of this section. Most of these items also appear in the Name Index where any relevant notes will be found.

	Ref	CE	BH
W1—Little Conduit, Cheapside	4L		
W2—Standard, Cheapside	4M		BH
W3—Clerk's Well	2H		
W4—Aldermanbury Well	4M	CE2	BH
W5—Aldermanbury Conduit	3N	CE1	
W6—Aldgate Well	4T		
W7—Hart Street Well	5T		BH
W8—Fenchurch Street Well	5S	CE2	
W9—Fleet Street Conduit	5H		BH
W10—Bishopsgate Well, Without	2R	CE1	BH
W11—Bishopsgate Well, Within	4R	CE2	BH
W12—Threadneedle Street Well	4Q	CE2	BH
W13—Stocks Market Conduit	4P	CE2	BH
W14—Cripplegate Conduit, Without	3M	CE2	BH
W15—Holborn Conduit	4J		BH
W16—St. Helen's Well	4R	CE2	BH
W17—Great Conduit, Cheapside	4N,5N	CE2	BH
Next to the conduit are some market stalls packed closely together in the middle of the street.			
W18—London Wall Conduit	3N	CE1	BH
W19—Bartholomew Close Conduit	3L		BH
W20—New Palace Yard fountain	7A		BH
Marked 'fountain' on Vertue's copy of the 'Agas' map.			
W21—conduit?	5B		BH
A conduit in this position is shown on *A survey of the conduits etc. to Whitehall and St. James*, 1718 (Crace Collection, British Museum).			
W22—well?	5B		
W23—conduit	5E		
W24—well	4S	CE2	
W25—boss	6S	CE2	BH
Coleman Street Conduit	(4P)	CE2	
Cornhill Well	(4Q)	CE2	
Gracechurch Street Conduit	(5R)	CE2	

(6) MISCELLANEOUS FEATURES

Item	Grid	Map	
Southwark Well	(8R)		BH
Standard, Cornhill	(4R)		
X1—cannon Presumably the site of a gun foundry.	6T	CE2	
X2—cannon Represents the site of the Gun-foundry, Houndsditch.	4T		BH
X3—washing	4A		BH
X4—washing	4B		
X5—washing	5U		
X6—washing	5V		
X7—windmill This post-mill is not shown on CE1. See also notes for X8.	2N		
X8—windmill This post-mill is shown in great detail on CE1. We can see the ladder providing access and the long tail pole used to turn the mill into the wind. The presence of a hooded sack-hoist indicates that the mill was used for grinding corn and not for draining the surrounding marsh. These windmills were situated on bone heaps. The three windmills X8, X9, X10 shown on the 'Agas' map are mentioned in a survey of the Manor of Finsbury, 1567. Only two are shown on CE1.	2P	CE1	
X9—windmill See also X8.	2P	CE1	
X10—windmill See also X8.	2P		
X11—water cans Tall wooden vessels hooped with osier, used by professional water carriers to take fresh water from house to house.	4N	CE2	BH

Item	Grid	Map	
X12—clock	6R	CE2	BH
X13—Eleanor Cross, Cheapside One of 12 memorial crosses erected by Edward I to mark the stages in the funeral procession of his queen, Eleanor. See also Charing Cross.	4M		
X14—kiln	1L		
X15—washing	3P		
X16—washing	3Q		BH
X17—crane	6N	CE2	BH
X18—crane	6N	CE2	BH
X19—crane	6P	CE2	BH
X20—windmill Named 'Mount Mill' on Morgan's map. Stow says it was on a hill called 'Mount Calvery'.	1L		
X21—crane	6U		BH
X22—cannons	6V		BH
X23—cannons	6V		BH
X24—cannon barrels	6U		BH
X25—kiln	5C		
X26—crane	6R	CE2	BH
X27—crane The top is shown on CE2.	6S	CE2	BH
X28—crane	6T		BH
X29—crane	6T		BH
X30—barrels	6S	CE2	BH
X31—cloth on tenter frame	3R	CE1	BH
X32—cloth on tenter frame	3S	CE1	BH
X33—cloth on tenter frame	3S	CE1	BH
X34—cloth on tenter frame	4S	CE1&2	BH
X35—cloth on tenter frame	4T		BH

Item	Grid	Map	
X36—washing	5U		
X37—tilt-yard The tilt-yard of Whitehall Palace. It is named Tilt-Yard on Vertue's map.	6B		BH
X38—stile and gate	7C		BH
X39—stile and gate	7C		BH
X40—laundry basket	4B		
X41—laundry basket	4A		
X42—cross It is mentioned by Stow: 'on the east side of this Red crosse streete, bee also diuers faire houses, up to the Crosse'. It is named on Vertue's map as 'Barbican Cross'.	2L		
X43—cross Stow mentions a cross at the junction of Old Street and Golden Lane. The 'Agas' map may therefore be in error.	2M		
X44—cross Represents the churchyard of St. Helen.	4R	CE2	BH
X45—cross Stands in the churchyard of St. Katherine Cree.	4S	CE2	BH
X46—cross This cross represents the churchyard of St. Gabriel Fenchurch.	5S	CE2	BH
X47—cross Represents the churchyard of St. Magnus the Martyr.	6R	CE2	
X48—cross This cross represents the churchyard of St. Andrew Hubbard.	6R	CE2	
X49—cross This cross is in the churchyard of St. Lawrence Poultney.	6Q	CE2	

X50—weathervane on Royal Exchange — 4Q — BH
Supposed to represent a grass-hopper, the crest of Sir Thomas Gresham, who was responsible for building the exchange.

X51—Martin Tower (Tower of London) — 6V — BH

X52—summer-house — 3Q — CE1
See notes under X144.

X53—laundry basket on cowl staff, being carried by two boys — 3Q — CE1

X54—laundry basket — 5V

X55—quintain or cross — 7J — BH
This looks like a cross on 'Agas' but on BH (which is probably more accurate) it would appear to be a quintain—an upright post with a crossbar turning on a pivot. Riders would aim to hit the broad end of the crossbar with a lance and then do their best to avoid being struck by the sandbag suspended from the other end of the arm.

X56—cross — 5U
This cross appears also on Vertue's map where it is named 'Minories Cross'.

X57—cross — 8R — BH
This cross represents the churchyard of St. Saviour, Southwark.

X58—haut-pas — 4L — BH
Built by a medieval goldsmith between his house and Goldsmiths' Hall.

X59—gateway — 5H — BH

X60—posts for tethering animals — 3J

X61—gateway — 5G — BH

X62—Smithfield Bars — 3K
Wooden posts marking the boundary of the City.

X63—railings — 3K — BH

X64—railings (Newgate Market) — 4K

X65—scaffold and gallows — 5T — BH

X66—cloth on tenter frame — 3N — CE1 — BH

X67—cloth on tenter frame — 3N — CE1 — BH

X68—cloth on tenter frame — 2Q, 2R — CE1 — BH

X69—cloth on tenter frame — 3Q, 3R — CE1 — BH

X70—Christ Church churchyard — 4K — BH

X71—railings — 8T, 8U

X72—Salt Tower (Tower of London) — 6V — BH

X73—house — 3N — CE1
This strange object on the 'Agas' map can be seen on CE1 to be a house, with a tower at its W. end and chimney set into its southern wall.

X74—target — 2S — CE1
This object and X75 are butts, built up of turf. Each would have had a target fastened to its face.

X75—target — 2S — CE1
See X74.

X76—gate — 3N — CE1
This gate and that marked X77 can be seen more clearly on CE1. They are referred to in Stow as marking the end of Postern Lane. See also Fore Street.

X77—gate — 3N — CE1
See X76.

X78—courtyard — 4L — BH
See St. Martin's-le-Grand (church)

X79—'Holbein' Gate, Whitehall Palace — 6B — BH

X80—smoke — 5U
Considering the thousands of chimneys in the City and the map-maker's eye for detail, it seems strange that so few are shown with smoke coming from them. Perhaps the mapmaker is indicating the site of a particularly smoky trade.

X81—smoke — 5V
See X80.

X82—pulpit cross — 2S — CE1
It is shown more clearly on CE1 with a cross on top. It is probably the pulpit of St. Mary Spital mentioned by Stow.

X83—St. Paul's Cross — 5L
'A pulpit cross of timber, mounted upon steps of stone and covered with lead, in which sermons are preached . . .' (Stow).

X84—?monument in churchyard — 5N — CE2
May be part of the nave.

X85—gallery — 5F — BH
A galleried corridor or passage leading from Arundel House to the riverside.

X86—cloisters — 5K — BH
The cloisters of Blackfriars priory (q.v.).

X87—gateway — 5K
A gateway into the priory of Blackfriars (q.v.).

X88—smoke — 7R
See X80.

X89—smoke — 7S
See X80.

X90—smoke — 7T
See X80.

X91—post — 5W
This could be a wayside cross.

X92—New Palace Yard (Westminster Palace) — 7A — BH

Entry	Grid	CE	BH
X93—gateway to St. Katherine's Hospital	6W		BH
X94—gateway	1Q	CE2	BH
X95—herring-busses or large market barges anchored in mid-stream	7W		BH
X96—gateway into New Palace Yard This gate, along with X97, X98 and X99, are all labelled as 'PALACE Gates' on Vertue's map.	7A		BH
X97—gate See also X96.	7A		BH
X98—gate See also X96.	8A		BH
X99—gate See also X96. This gate has an irregular outline which may indicate a ruined wall.	8A		BH
X100—Jewel Tower (Westminster Palace)	8A		BH
X101—fountain	6B		BH
X102—The Cockpit, Whitehall Palace	6A		BH
X103—Old Palace Yard One of the old courtyards of Westminster Palace (q.v.).	8A		BH
X104—House of Commons	7A		BH
X105—House of Lords	8A		BH
X106—houses Described by Norden on his plan as 'the Park Lodgings'.	6A		BH
X107—garden Named as 'Spring Garden' by Vertue on his copy of the 'Agas' map.	5A,5B		BH
X108—water mill	8V		BH
X109—path Although shown as a large thoroughfare, a map of Horsleydown, 1544, shows a large field with a path crossing it in much the same way as BH.	8W		BH
X110—Beer House No. 1 See notes in Name Index.	8V		BH
X111—water mill	8U		BH
X112—bridge This bridge is also shown on a map of Horsleydown dated 1544.	8V		BH
X113—stream See also X114.	8U		BH
X114—stream This and stream X113 are shown on Morgan's map. A third stream crossed Tooley Street near the Bridge House, according to Morgan, but the 'Agas' map does not show it. These streams were in effect open sewers.	8V		BH
X115—St. Olave's Watergate A wharf belonging to the City of London.	8S		BH
X116—Pudding Mill A water mill. The mill pond can be seen just south of this building.	7J		BH
X117—ponds	8M,8N		BH
X118—kennels Four rows of kennels are shown, each holding several dogs. The mastiffs were bred and trained here to attack bulls and bears for sport.	8M,8N		BH
X119—Beer House No. 3 See notes in Name Index.	5C		BH
X120—The Great Hall, Whitehall Palace Built by Cardinal Wolsey in 1528.	6B		BH
X121—Barbican (Tower) See notes in Name Index.	2L		BH
X122—Black House See Black House in Name Index.	3R	CE1	BH
X123—Giardin di Piero See Giardin di Piero in Name Index.	3R	CE1	BH
X124—gatehouse This is the gatehouse to St. John's Priory (q.v.).	2J		BH
X125—Chapel Royal, Whitehall Palace	6B		BH
X126—cloisters Cloisters of the former Priory of Greyfriars.	4K		BH
X127—Great Close Tennis Court, Whitehall Palace	6A		BH
X128—King Street Gate One of the main gate-houses to the Palace of Whitehall.	6A		
X129—haut-pas	5K		BH
X130—Little Close Tennis Court, Whitehall Palace	6A		BH
X131—water gate On the site of the present York water gate.	5C		
X132—Privy Garden, Whitehall Palace It is called 'Queens Garden' on Vertue's map.	6B		BH
X133—Beauchamp Tower (Tower of London)	6U		BH
X134—Middle Tower (Tower of London)	6U		BH
X135—Byward Tower (Tower of London)	6U		BH
X136—Wakefield Tower (Tower of London)	6V		BH
X137—Bell Tower (Tower of London)	6U		BH
X138—Devereux Tower (Tower of London)	6U		BH

X139—St. Thomas's Tower (Tower of London) — 6U — BH

X140—Cradle Tower (Tower of London) — 6V

X141—Lanthorn Tower (Tower of London) — 6V

X142—pond, partly enclosed by a fence. — 2N — CE1 — BH

X143—stream — 2N — CE1
It is only shown running beside Chiswell Street on the 'Agas' map but on CE1 it can be seen following the lane beside the windmills (X8, X9).

X144—summer house — 3Q — CE1
This house, the one due E. (X52) and a third (looking like a beehive) shown on CE1 to the N. of X144, may well be the summer houses mentioned by Stow. The building of elaborate garden houses in the rural suburbs was very popular in the 16th century.

X145—Bethlehem Hospital Chapel — 3R — CE1 — BH

X146—bridge — 3Q — CE2 — BH
A covered bridge, over Deep Ditch, leading from Moor Field to Bethlehem Hospital.

X147—garden — 3P,3Q — CE1 — BH
This garden and X148 were part of the land of Winchester House, Broad Street (q.v.).

X148—garden — 4P,4Q — CE1 — BH
See X147.

X149—drainage ditches — 8H,7G — BH

X150—pergola — 5P — CE2 — BH
This may be the garden of Bucklersbury House which Stow describes as 'the great stone building yet in part remaining on the south side of Bucklersbury'. The stone building is not shown. — BH

X151—Great Open Tennis Court ('The Brake' or Balloon Court), Whitehall Palace. — 6A

X152—crane — 6P — CE2 — BH

X153—gateway — 5F — BH

X154—gateway (known as the Ship Gate) — 4G

X155—tree — 5F

X156—gateway — 8S — BH
Possibly the entrance to St. Thomas's Hospital (q.v.) but may well be one of the arched gates to Lewes Inn, described by Stow.

X157—Dormitory of the Savoy Hospital, with octagonal lantern. See Savoy Palace. — 5E — BH

X158—enclosure — 3K — BH
An enclosure built outside the west front of St. Bartholomew's Church, possibly to prevent horses and cattle from straying into the building. Referred to as 'le cheyne' in 1544. See also St. Bartholomew the Great.

X159—Drapers' Garden — 4P — CE2 — BH

X160—alley — 5T — BH
Later known as Northumberland Alley.

X161—turret — 5J — BH

X162—Brass Mount (Tower of London) — 6V — BH

X163—tower (unnamed) — 6V — BH

X164—tower (unnamed) — 6V — BH

X165—Legge's Mount (Tower of London) — 6U — BH

X166—gateway to the precinct of Westminster Abbey — 7A — BH

X167—gateway to the nunnery of St. Mary Clerkenwell — 2J — BH

X168—gateway into St. Paul's precinct — 5L — BH

X169—milk churn — 3V — BH

X170—fountain — 3Q — CE1 — BH
In the garden of Winchester House, Broad Street.

X171—Charnel-house and chapel of St. Edmund the Bishop and Mary Magdalen — 2R — CE1 — BH

X172—byre — 8M — BH
Probably a byre where the bulls were kept.

X173—Prior's garden — 5K — BH
Part of the former Priory of the Black Friars (q.v.).

X174—Bloody Tower (Tower of London) — 6U — BH

X175—wall — 3C — BH
The remains of the wall which had formerly enclosed the hospital of St. Giles.

X176—St. Bartholomew the Less Churchyard — 3K — BH

X177—chapel — 2K — BH
Shown in the centre of the Charterhouse churchyard, now Charterhouse Square.

X178—Prior's garden — 3L — BH
Part of the former Priory of St. Bartholomew (q.v.).

X179—Bartholomew Fair, Site of — 3K — BH
The area between the church of St. Bartholomew the Great and Long Lane was the site of the annual Bartholomew Fair, which until

Elizabethan times was the most
important cloth fair in England.

X180—wherry with spritsail and oars proceeding downstream 8B BH

X181—ten-oared galley towing the Royal Barge upstream. The galley has 12 oars on BH. 6K BH

X182—The Royal Barge proceeding upstream 6L BH
This tilt-boat with its long tunnel-like canopy, is being towed by a galley and steered with a long sweep instead of a rudder (only visible on BH). The Queen (either Elizabeth or Mary) is surrounded by halberdiers.

X183—shallop proceeding upstream 7L

X184—timber barge alongside 6Q

X185—herring-buss in Billingsgate Dock 6S

X186—three-masted deep sea 'bark' discharging cargo in Billingsgate Dock 6S BH

X187—three-masted deep sea 'bark' discharging cargo in Billingsgate Dock 6S

X188—herring-buss alongside at Billingsgate 7S BH

X189—barges anchored in the Upper Pool 7S,7T BH

X190—galleons anchored in the Upper Pool 7V,7W BH

X191—scales for weighing meal?
Situated in the quadrangle of Leadenhall Market (q.v.) and mentioned by Stow. The object may possibly be a well. 5R CE2 BH

X192—Mopp Gate (entrance to Holy Trinity Priory) 4S CE2 BH

X193—watch-tower 6P CE2
This was situated at the S. end of the hall of the Steelyard (q.v.). Several such towers (perhaps originally built by merchants to look out for their returning ships) existed in 16th-century London. More clearly shown on CE2.

X194—Coldharbour Tower (Tower of London). 6V BH

X195—tower 4L BH
see: St. Leonard Foster Lane; St. Martins-le-Grand (Church). This tower is not shown on Vertue's map.

X196—tower 6R CE2
Probably meant to represent St. Martin Orgar (q.v.). Vertue's map does not show a tower in this position nor does he show one where St. Martin is known to have been.

X197—tower 5N CE2 BH
No church is known to have stood on this site. Vertue's map does not show this tower.

X198—tower 4T
This tower would seem to be here by error. The tower does not appear on BH or on Vertue's map.

X199—tower 4P CE2 BH
Referred to as Grocers' Hall Tower on Leake's map.

X200—chapel 5R CE2 BH
This may be Leadenhall Chapel. If so, it is shown a little way S. of its true position on all 3 maps. It was situated on the E. side of the main quadrangle. On the other hand it may be the chapel of a great house on the W. side of

---

Lime Street which Stow describes as having been 'lately' taken down.

X201—bowling alley, Whitehall Palace 6A BH

X202—passage between Whitehall Palace and St. James's Park 6A BH

X203—Pheasant Court, Whitehall Palace 6A BH

X204—Cockpit lodgings, Whitehall Palace 6A BH

X205—King's Head alehouse
Not part of Whitehall Palace 6A BH

X206—Privy Gallery, Whitehall Palace 6B BH

X207—Whitehall Palace kitchens 6B BH

X208—preaching place, Whitehall Palace 6B BH

X209—The Court, Whitehall Palace 6B BH

X210—Stone Gallery, Whitehall Palace 'Agas' shows the gable end only. 6B

X211—Princes Lodgings, Whitehall Palace 6B BH

X212—Council Chamber, Whitehall Palace 6B BH

X213—orchard, Whitehall Palace 6B BH

X214—?building under construction 6B BH

X215—Pudding Mill Stream 8J BH

X216—Castell upon the Hope Inn
One of the Southwark stewhouses (i.e. a brothel). Referred to in 1559 as the 'Castell on the hoope'. Later the site of the Anchor public house. 8P BH

X217—water mill 7P BH